Riding on Beverly Beach, Oregon

WILD PIGS

THE MOUNTAIN BIKE ADVENTURE GUIDE
TO THE PACIFIC COAST

John Zilly

Photos by Wade Praeger

Adventure Press
Seattle

Adventure Press
P.O. Box 14059
Seattle, Washington 98114

Copyediting: Ella M. David
Maps: John Zilly
Photography: Wade Praeger and John Zilly
Cover photos: Wade Praeger

Cover: On the left, touring south near Otter Bay, Oregon; on the right, mountain biking near the John Muir Woods on Mount Tamalpais in Marin County, California

Library of Congress Catalog Card Number: 94-78208
John Zilly
Wild Pigs: The Mountain Bike Adventure Guide to the Pacific Coast

ISBN: 1-881583-05-8

 Printed on recycled paper with soy-based ink

For Angela

ACKNOWLEDGMENTS

Thank you to all those who helped me with this book and encouraged
me along the way. *Wild Pigs* wouldn't have happened without you.
For their assistance and contribution, special thanks to Nancy Penrose,
Angela Castañeda, Tom Zilly, Jane Noland, Mark Klebanoff, Mary
Anne Christy, Ruth Flanders, Jens Molbak, Blair Carleton, John
Ensinck, Jeff Dalto, John Livengood, Marcelo Truffat, Jeanine
Spence, Rachael Hannah, Eric Cobb, the late Carl Replogle, the Scott
Family, and to Wade for his brilliant photographs.

And to my riding partners, Wade Praeger, Peter Zilly, David Graves,
and Binkley—a veritable rolling focus group—thank you for all the
input, support, and friendship.

OVERVIEW MAP

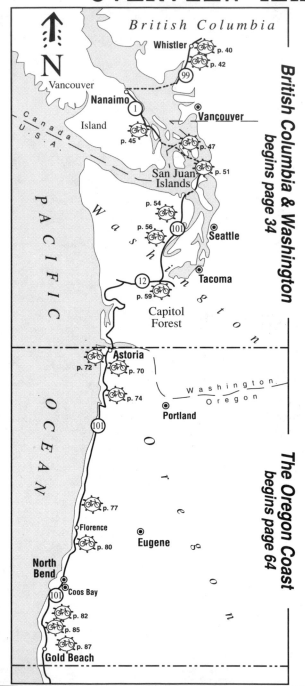

British Columbia

Whistler ○ p. 40

p. 42

99

Vancouver

Nanaimo 1

Island

Vancouver

p. 45

p. 47

San Juan Islands

p. 51

p. 54

p. 56

101

Seattle

12

Tacoma

p. 59

Capitol Forest

Astoria

p. 72

p. 70

Washington
Oregon

p. 74

Portland

101

Oregon

p. 77

Florence

p. 80

Eugene

North Bend

Coos Bay

101

p. 82

p. 85

p. 87

Gold Beach

British Columbia & Washington
begins page 34

The Oregon Coast
begins page 64

PACIFIC OCEAN

Canada
U.S.A.

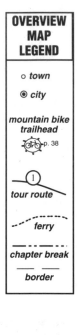

OVERVIEW MAP LEGEND

○ *town*

◉ *city*

mountain bike trailhead

p. 38

1

tour route

- - - - *ferry*

— · · — *chapter break*

— — — *border*

OVERVIEW MAP

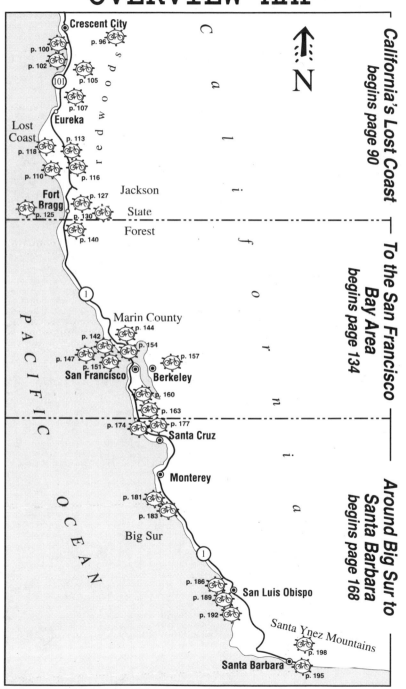

Crescent City

p. 96

p. 100

p. 102

101

p. 105

p. 107

Eureka

Lost Coast

p. 113

p. 118

p. 110

p. 116

Jackson

State

Forest

Fort Bragg

p. 125

p. 127

p. 130

p. 140

N

California's Lost Coast
begins page 90

1

Marin County

p. 144

p. 142

p. 154

p. 147

p. 157

p. 151

San Francisco

Berkeley

p. 160

p. 163

p. 174

p. 177

Santa Cruz

Monterey

p. 181

p. 183

Big Sur

1

p. 186

p. 189

San Luis Obispo

p. 192

Santa Ynez Mountains

p. 198

Santa Barbara

p. 195

To the San Francisco
Bay Area
begins page 134

Around Big Sur to
Santa Barbara
begins page 168

PACIFIC OCEAN

California

CONTENTS

RIDES BY DIFFICULTY

BE RESPONSIBLE FOR YOURSELF

The author and publisher of *Wild Pigs: The Mountain Bike Adventure Guide to the Pacific Coast* disclaim and are in no way responsible or liable for the consequences of using this guide, unless you have a good time.

1. *Mountain bicycling and bicycle touring are dangerous:* Cyclists can get lost, become injured, or suffer from serious fatigue. The difficulty of the trails described in this guide and the level of skill and experience required to ride safely on the trails are subjective. Each rider must assess his or her preparedness for any trail in light of his or her own skills, training, experience, and equipment.

2. *Trail and road conditions are subject to change without notice.* The information contained in this book, as of the date of publication, was as accurate as possible. But conditions on these routes change quickly: storms, logging, stream revisions, land slides, trail and road construction, and development, among other things, can drastically alter the landscape and its trails, in some cases making the trails dangerous and/or unridable.

3. *Do not ride on private property unless you are sure the landowner has granted permission.* Some of the rides described in this guide cross private land. Do not conclude that the owner has granted you permission to use the trails. If the property has no posted signs, and you are not sure of its status, you should obtain permission from the owner before proceeding.

4. *Public jurisdictions may change rules at any time.* Most of the rides described in this guide are located on public land. The rides in this book were legal at the time of publication, but in the future land managers may exclude bicycles, regulate bicycle use, or require permits. Understanding the laws as they change is up to you.

The author assumes absolutely no responsibility for these or any other problems that may occur while cycling or otherwise, nor should he. Hey kids, be responsible for yourselves and the land you are using.

BE COOL TO THE EARTH

It's easy to be a cynical bicyclist these days. Each year, thousands of miles of trails are closed to mountain bicycles, trails that conform to multi-use standards, trails where mountain bikers are the majority use, trails that entire families enjoy by bicycle. Meanwhile, every bike commuter and bicycle tourist has been yelled at by an obnoxious driver. And you're lucky if you've only been yelled at.

Despite abuse from drivers and evil, fisheye looks from non-biking trail users, almost nothing you can do outside the house is as environmentally sound as bicycling. Bicyclists have always been part of the conservation movement. Commuters who cycle to work deserve much green praise; vacationers who choose bicycling deserve environmental kudos. Now, new scientific studies show that, on dirt trails, a mountain bicycle may displace less sediment than a hiker. Let me repeat and reword for those stuck in the previous paradigm: wheels have the same—*or less*—impact as boots on soft-surface trails. Tell everyone you know, including land managers and legislators. People need to remember, "Oh yeah, bicycling is good for the earth."

This doesn't mean that we, the martyr cyclists, are so pure that we don't do anything wrong. Sometimes we do. It's our responsibility to lead by example. We need not only to think green but also to act green as well: just mount-

Bicycle and gull tracks in the sand

ing a bicycle isn't enough. We need to build and maintain trails, clean littered roadways, educate new riders, use environmentally sound chain lubes, and ride responsibly and safely. A few renegade mountain bicyclists skid and thrash; a few tourists heave banana peels and blown inner tubes into the ditch. We can't continue to do this stuff. We need to be as clean and pure as our trusty bikes or more trails will be closed, and bicycles will begin turning up in museums instead of being the centerpiece of the environmental movement.

WILD PIGS

One hundred years ago along the Pacific coast, people raised pigs in their back yards; some even kept them in their front yards. Then somewhere along this century's footpath, raising pigs went out of style, pork went from hip to hick (the cultural view of history). Or perhaps the profitability went out of pigs (the economic view of history). Whatever the precise change, one day pig owners began unlatching their gates and shooing the pigs out. As the new no-pig style spread, brooms swished and poked, muddy boots kicked and pushed, and lots of pigs were left wondering what to do.

Being smart and resourceful, the pigs headed for the hills to live on their own. Generations later these once-domestic animals, kicked out into the wild to fend for themselves, had done just that—enthusiastically. The pigs had become abundant, as were stories of their exploits. North of San Francisco, wild pigs roamed the chaparral faces of Mount Tamalpais, chasing hikers down the Hoo-koo-e-koo Trail. After a couple hours of rooting in the hills of Montana de Oro near San Luis Obispo, they ate rattlesnakes for dessert. In southern Oregon, pigs munched their way up the Rogue River valley, flossing their teeth with poison oak. Each time hikers complained.

Eventually the sad day arrived. With guns blasting, the pig eradication programs began. Although only a few pigs survived, they live on in a spiritual sense. Click on your imagination here: we can learn from those pigs while we sit in our living rooms, listening to classic rock stations, paging through cycling magazines, watching clouds speed across the sky through double-pane windows. Kick yourself out of the house. Get out on your bike and learn about enthusiasm and adventure, mystery and power. Go ahead, be a pig!

Imagine a cycling trip along the Pacific coast: sea stacks and gulls, the wild coast range, redwood and wind-sculpted cypress, winding roads, dirt trails, endless views, lighthouses, beaches. Pretty cool picture. *Wild Pigs* is a mountain biker's dream book: over forty-five great mountain-bike trails for all ages and abilities from Whistler, British Columbia, to Santa Barbara, California. The maps, trail descriptions, elevation profiles, and photos describe each trail like it's the one you ride every weekend. Bicycle touring down the coast is incredible as well, so I've included everything a mountain bicyclist needs to tour the Pacific coast: maps, elevation profiles, and Quick Facts (campgrounds, restaurants, bed and breakfasts, bakeries, bike shops, and more) for the entire 1600 miles of roadway along the Pacific coast. Whether you want to go to the Pacific coast to mountain bike on trails or tour the coast highways, or both, this is your book.

So when you adventure across a steep chaparral slope far from home, give yourself a pat on the back for being a wild and adventurous pig. And remember, the eyes of wild pigs may be watching as you glide by.

USING THIS GUIDE
Mountain Bicycling

Wild Pigs contains over 45 mountain bike rides between Whistler, British Columbia, and Santa Barbara, California. The rides are organized from north to south within each of the five sections: **British Columbia & Washington (p. 34); The Oregon Coast (p. 64); California's Lost Coast (p. 90); To the San Francisco Bay Area (p. 134);** and **Around Big Sur to Santa Barbara (p. 168).** The rides included span all ability levels and are located on or close to the official *Wild Pigs* touring route for the Pacific coast.

The information for each mountain bike ride is straightforward and easy to use. Here's a rundown of the information provided.

Difficulty rating

Each ride is rated from **1 to 4 wheels,** depending on the length of the trip, the hills, and the level of riding skill required. Find this rating at the top of each ride to select an appropriate ride.

Easy: Anyone can ride a one-wheel ride; it isn't much different from riding on a paved country road. These rides are short, not very hilly, and stay on wide, well-packed riding surfaces.

Moderate: A two-wheel ride traverses primarily dirt roads, jeep trails (rough dirt roads), and occasionally easy trails, also referred to as "single track." These rides are longer and have more elevation gain than one-wheelers. Although the riding isn't technical, short sections may have to be walked.

Difficult: During a three-wheel ride you will encounter dirt roads, jeep trails, and certainly some single-track. These rides are longer, have steep or long climbs, and cross tricky spots that will likely require pushing your bike.

Most Difficult: If a ride is long, has lots of steep or grueling hills, and is full of technical riding, I have rated it four wheels. Many riders may have to push or carry their bikes for stretches during a four-wheel ride. These rides can be dangerous and exhausting. A high level of fitness and advanced or expert mountain-bike skills are recommended.

Ride statistics

Checklist Trip distance and riding surface are noted for each ride. Rides are labeled **Out and Back**, **Loop**, or **One Way**. **One Way** means that the ride does not finish at the same place it began.

Duration The duration is listed with some reservation since everything depends on the rider's skill, stamina, and map-reading abilities. Use this figure as a very general guideline.

Hill factor The hill factor describes the difficulty and number of hills that will be encountered. The elevations marked on each map identify the high, low, and starting point for each ride. Climbs are noted in the ride description.

Skill level Rides are rated beginner, intermediate, advanced, or expert depending on the technical demands of the trail. This rates the minimum bike-handling abilities a cyclist needs for the ride.

Maps Maps are mandatory, unless you enjoy bivouacking with your bicycle. I've listed the best map to use for each area.

Season The best time of year for this trail. Don't ride on trails that are closed or liable to be damaged in wet weather.

User density This describes who uses the trail and how intensive the use is.

Explorability Listed as low, medium, or high, this rating indicates the number of other trails in the vicinity. A high rating means there are lots of trails to be explored. Don't get lost.

In sunshine near Point Reyes, California

Ride descriptions

Teaser Rides begin with a paragraph that paints a picture of the journey, the wonders and challenges. May ride magic follow.

Ride The primary reason to have this book in hand is to get to the trailhead and then stay on the trail. This section contains a detailed description of the terrain—up or down, left or right. These paragraphs note the **mileage** at forks in the trail, hills, and other significant landmarks. Here are a few of the conventions I use while describing the rides. "**Stay on the main trail/ road**" means that other trails may exit from the main trail— use good judgment to stay on the obvious main line. The word "**Whoa**" signifies a dangerous section of trail or a turn easily missed, and warns the rider to pay close attention. When one trail deadends at another forcing a 90° turn either right or left, the resulting three-way intersection is described as a "**T.**" Other three-way intersections are described interchangeably as "**forks**" or "**the trail divides**." When two trails cross, the result is usually refered to as a "**4-way intersection**".

Trail maps and elevation profiles

Maps The bike route is defined by a series of arrows. Find the trailhead using the written instructions on the map. The beginning of the ride is designated by a small bike 🚲 and the end by an arrow with a line →|. Elevations (in feet above sea level) mark the high point, the low point, and the starting point of each ride. For more map information, refer to the Micro Legend located at the top of each map.

Getting there Directions to the trailhead are located on the map for each ride.

Elevations Located under some maps, you'll also find elevation profiles that show the climbing involved in a particular ride. If a ride does not have an elevation profile, no climbs exist that gain sufficient elevation to make an elevation graph useful. This does not mean, however, that the ride lacks hills. A ride with no graph may be quite hilly, with lots of short hills that don't register on an elevation profile. Check the "**Hill factor**" rating at the beginning of the ride for a description.

Crossing the Navarro River near Elk, California

USING THIS GUIDE
Touring

Of all the touring I've done, I have never found a stretch of road quite as wonderful as the Pacific coast, which I define as the road between Whistler, British Columbia and Santa Barbara, California. Sometimes it rains too hard, sometimes the woodchip trucks drive too close, and sometimes the hills appear too frequently. But more often you'll be shading your eyes to watch whales migrate, reading a book on the beach, or riding a tailwind past another lighthouse.

If you want to use this book as a touring guide, the **Tour Guide** maps, the **Quick Facts** pages, and the section **Preludes** are all you need to tour the entire coast. The best thing about each touring section is you, the reader. You experience your *own* tour, rather than follow someone else's. You are the one who knows if you want to ride 20 miles or 120 miles, on dirt or pavement, and whether you are traveling for five days or five months. The five geographic sections make *Wild Pigs* easy to use. Here's what you'll find in each section about coast touring:

Overview map   These maps, located on pages 35, 65, 91, 135, and 169, help you locate the stretch of the coast described in that section. The area covered in that section is highlighted.

Prelude   Each prelude, located on pages 35, 65, 91, 135, and 169, tells the story of an experience I had while touring the Pacific coast. These narratives put a real face on bicycling the trails, roads, and highways between Whistler, B.C., and Santa Barbara, Calif. I hope they communicate the essence of this book— combining mountain biking with bicycle touring. I hope, too, that the stories ignite a spark of enthusiasm to be a pig, to travel to the coast with your bicycle and explore.

Quick Facts   The Quick Facts pages report on the nuts and bolts of Pacific coast bicycle touring, such as bed & breakfasts (B&Bs), campgrounds, places to eat and drink, sights, supplementary books and maps, bike shops, and other oddities. Enjoy.

Tour Guide   If you are touring, these two pages are where it all happens. Reasonable questions are fielded: how far is the next town? Where are the hills and how tall are they? When can we stop and camp? Don't you think it's a nice night for a B&B? Is there a bike mechanic on this road? With this information (and your own wits thrown in for good measure), touring down the coast is a breeze. The Tour Guide also includes elevation profiles along the edge of the map, so you can judge the day ahead by the number of climbs as well as the overall distance.

Shoe storage at Sandy Cove Inn, Inverness, California (page 138)

THE EFFICIENT TOURIST

Doing the touring/mountain bike jig

If you have thought about touring the entire coast and mountain biking along the way, you've probably wondered about the logistics of such a trip. **Touring on a mountain bike:** it's true, you'll make better time with a traditional, dropped-bar touring bike, but the comfort of a mountain bike—more cushion from the fat tires, the upright riding position that causes less neck strain and allows you to see more of the coast, and the ease of gearing and braking—outweighs the disadvantages. **Tires:** I recommend riding on high-pressure slicks when touring and carrying a rear off-road tire for mountain biking. Some riders don't mind the extra noise and resistance of touring on knobbies; purists, on the other hand, tour on slicks and carry two extra tires to "do the mountain biking right." **Stashing your stuff:** No one wants to mountain bike with pannier bags, but no one wants to leave them behind, either. Some people feel comfortable putting their bags in the tent while they go mountain biking. If you don't, ask a ranger if you can leave your bags in the visitor's center or ranger station. You can also try stashing your bags off the road where no one will see them. If you are in a group, you can always draw straws to see who stays back to watch the gear.

The Neat tourist

Remember what I said about being a pig? I meant it metaphorically, in the sense of get out there, do it, feel the mystery. When staying at a B&B, though, don't try to emulate the habits of a real pig. Bicycling can be grimy. It's not cool to track dirt through a B&B, bounce your greasy pannier bags on the bedspread, gouge wood floors with cycling cleats, or use the towels for bike maintenance.

Being neat and considerate is a noble pursuit whether you are in a B&B or out on the open road. Keep your bags neat and tied down properly or you will lose your gear. A clean bike, free of road grit, will provide a quieter, more efficient ride; a clean campsite will help keep the raccoons and skunks at bay. Don't litter, be discreet about where you go to the bathroom, and obey the traffic.

Partners

When you decide to tour with someone, you had better be good friends. Bicycle touring is like being married, except you're attatched to your touring partner 24 hours each day—no break. The pressures of traveling can be exhausting, combined with the physical stresses of riding a bike all day, the result may be disorienting and explosive. During the hard times, all decisions—from where to camp to what type of bread to buy—seem like possible tour-breakers.

Siuslaw River at Florence, Oregon

Partners, by definition, are equals, and this is the way touring should be. Each person in the group should feel equal—in fitness, in equipment, in the way you want to tour—or insoluble problems can erupt. As usual, communication is the key. If it's not possible to be completely equal, the inequalities or personal differences should be thoroughly discussed early in the trip planning. To avoid problems, some partners form some sort of government, for example "I make the decisions one day, you make them the next." Travelers sometimes divide up the chores; others just make it up as they go along. Obviously, these are general suggestions. The point is that it's smart to discuss this before the trip begins.

Eating

Eating properly is a critical element of a successful tour. Take advantage of the grocery stores along the route and buy a variety of fresh food each day. Leave enough time at the end of the day to prepare it. Due to the increased stresses on your body, one of the great pleasures of touring is eating as much as you want. When I tour, my daily intake jumps from 2200 calories to 5000 calories. During the first few days of a tour I find it nearly impossible to stuff all that food down my gullet. But if I didn't force myself to eat, my partners would feed me to the next woodchip truck driver because I'd be far too ornery.

Touring fatigue

On long tours, you're bound to have those days when you don't feel like riding, or talking to anyone, or eating. Although these marshmallow days seem inevitable, there are some strategies to avoid them. First, you don't have to plunge into an epic tour right away, or ever. Find an interesting stretch of road and spend a weekend or a week, then drive to a trail for some mountain biking. Be creative.

Second, learn how to draft efficiently (ride directly behind your partner to avoid pumping against the wind) and then trade off drafting with your riding partner. This allows you to hold a conversation and conserve energy. Occasionally, though, it's refreshing to ride alone for the day to cleanse yourself of your partner's bile. Don't ride too hard: reading on the beach, cooking a fine camp dinner, and fireside conversations are all elements of a great tour, so don't ruin them by pushing too hard during the day.

What to bring

Everyone tours differently; some like to carry gallons of milk and musical instruments, others enjoy telling stories about how little they packed (although they leave out the part about how cold they were). Other than the mandatory rain jacket, warm hat, cycling shorts and gloves, and helmet, you are on your own. One method of selecting gear is to put everything you think you need in a pile, and then use two principles: **1.** Don't overpack your pannier bags (leave room for food). **2.** You can always send stuff home or buy stuff along the way.

Weather and tour time

The weather on the Pacific coast is unpredictable, so you won't regret carrying a rain jacket. But a little planning will mean you have to use it less. From May through mid-November the prevailing winds blow north to south. Planning to ride south to north, and bucking the wind, is foolish. As far as the weather goes, August and September are the favorites. I like touring the coast from mid-September through the end of October because I think it provides an optimum combination of good weather and moderate traffic, especially RV traffic.

Camping

Camping is one of the great delights during a Pacific coast bicycle tour. First, there are lots and lots of campgrounds scattered up and down the coast, and they are almost always within an easy day's ride. Second, many of the campgrounds on the coast have areas dedicated to muscle-powered travelers. These "hiker/biker" areas cost much less than regular camp sites. Campgrounds generally won't turn hikers or bicyclists away, so these sites never really fill up. Finally, much of the fun of a tour is sitting around a picnic table lit by a candle and trading stories with others cyclists.

Humbug Mountain State Park, Oregon

SAFETY

Mountain bicycling

The biggest safety concern while cycling in the mountains is the header, the endo, the cartwheel, the flip—and landing on your head is not cool. Avoid crashing by maintaining control and riding at moderate speeds. Stay away from trails beyond your ability. To minimize the effects of a crash, always wear a helmet, carry a first-aid kit, ride with a friend, and slow down.

The danger of mountain biking isn't just the big crash, though. A simple mechanical failure, a sore knee, or exhaustion can strand you miles from the trailhead and force an unplanned night in the woods. If you don't have the proper supplies—like food, extra clothes, plenty of water, and a light—you could be in trouble. I know some people who spent a night under a log. Since they only had T-shirts, they kept themselves warm with a blanket of dirt. Not a pretty sight. It's best to be prepared.

Mountain bikers can be dangerous to themselves—flying off cliffs, bobbing down streams, launching into large trees—but they can also be dangerous to other trail users. Only your mom cares if you fly off the edge of a canyon, but when you careen around blind corners, everyone cares. Out-of-control riders are the reason so many trails have been closed to mountain bikes.

The safety problem arises because mountain bikes are quiet and can travel more quickly than pedestrians. To alleviate a mishap, mountain bicyclists *must* ride as if a small child is around every corner. On long downhill sections, attach a bell to your bike, so you sound like a cow and other trail users can hear you approaching. Mountain bicyclists should always yield the trail to all other users: hikers, equestrians, motorcyclists, and other bicyclists. The only other alternative would be to close or segregate trails, and both leave mountain bicyclists with fewer miles to ride and less beautiful land to enjoy.

Touring

While touring, concrete and automobiles become part of the safety discussion. Avoiding skin contact with both seems to be the best piece of advice. When you ride on the road, your bicycle is considered a vehicle and liable to the same laws as all other vehicles. Obeying those laws will greatly improve your chances.

There are a number of specific circumstances which are quite dangerous to bicycle tourists. Touring the coast, you will cross numerous **bridges**. Many of these bridges are narrow; some have treacherous metal grates. In almost every case, it's best to ride or walk on the raised path off the car deck. **Trucks and RVs** are another problem. Although the noise and wind turbulence they create are unnerving, if you hold on to your wits and ride a straight line you should be fine. **Tunnels** are also scary. Luckily, there are just two tunnels on the coast, both in

Highway 101 near Cape Perpetua, Oregon

Oregon—one just south of Arch Cape and one between Yachats and Florence. Other hazards include whipping crosswinds, thieves, and helmet hair. In all these circumstances, it's best to plan ahead: know where you'll go if a truck comes too close, know how you'll lock your bike while shopping, and try shaving your head to avoid hair problems.

Losing the way

Cyclists get lost all the time, usually because they are trying to hammer too hard. If you become lost while touring, it's usually just an inconvenience. The best advice for the disoriented tourist is to carry a lot of maps and ask, ask, ask for directions. But it's a completely different story if you get lost out in the mountains—no one speaks your language. Getting lost in the woods while riding a bike is easier than you might think. Stop and pay attention to your surroundings; watch the lay of the land; review the maps.

To avoid getting lost: **1.** Gain an adequate knowledge of the area before leaving. **2.** Bring a map, compass, and the skills to use them. **3.** Note the turns and avoid theoretical shortcuts. **4.** Stay home if severe weather is forecast. **5.** Follow people who know the trail; beware of people who *think* they know the trail.

Use good sense and stay on the main trail: faint trails, animal paths, abandoned railroad grades, and logging roads are everywhere. Your brain must sift through all the information— maps and trail descriptions, the sun, your compass, the lay of the land—and you must decide not to get lost. If you do find yourself lost in the woods, don't panic. Put on all your warm clothes, then try to relax and think with your cortex rather than your thalamus.

Rear rack breakdown: catastrophic failure or minor repair?

Minimize the risk

- Always wear a helmet.
- Never bike alone.
- **In the mountains:** Avoid violent speed experiences and out-of-control riding. Watch out for other trail users, sharp bends in the trail, ruts, roots, rocks, fallen trees, cliffs, and animals.
- **On the road:** On winding descents watch for gravel on the road, tight curves, and narrow shoulders. Always be aware of driveways, intersections, and parked cars (doors can open at any time).
- Carry a good first-aid kit and know how to use it. Toss in sunscreen, a lighter, and a pocket knife, too.
- Wear eye protection.
- Drink plenty of water: at least two quarts of water per day.
- Always, always bring along a good map. A compass, a cycle computer, and an altimeter won't hurt, either. Don't play *Journey to the Center of the Earth.*
- Carry extra clothes no matter how nice the weather is when you leave (hat, gloves, jacket, long underwear, wind pants), food (energy bars are good; date bars are better), and a flashlight.
- Make sure someone in the group has the proper tools and knows how to use them.
- Hunting season? Be careful: A bullet hole in your new jersey is a sure way to ruin the ride.

TRAILSIDE REPAIRS

Whoa. When you bicycle into the backcountry, damage to your bike can mean a long walk with a bike on your shoulder. Always carry a tool kit so you can fix anything from nine flat tires to a broken chain. Sometimes you need some imagination to concoct short-term fixes for problems: fill your flat tire with pine cones, take some links out of your chain if your derailleur explodes. When I rode around the United States a number of years ago, I found that almost anything could be repaired, one way or another, if I had the four essentials—duct tape, vice grips, super glue, bailing wire (these four items also kept my '69 Dodge Coronet running for years). Of course some problems are even too catastrophic for the big four essentials. You may find yourself ten miles out in the woods with a broken frame, a pretzelled wheel, or some other catastrophic failure, and unfortunately there's not a pannier bag big enough to carry that amount of duct tape—thus the advice to take along water, food, flashlight, lighter, and extra clothes.

If you have a breakdown while touring, you probably won't have to spend a night in the woods, but the trip will be a lot more enjoyable if you don't have to hitch a ride from the next car. As with mountain biking, the first principle of fixing a problem is imagination. Here is a suggested list of tools. But remember: everyone's bike is different, so you should customize this list so it makes sense for your bike.

Recommended tools for road or dirt

- pump
- patch kit
- extra tube
- tire irons
- extra spokes
- freewheel remover
- spoke wrench
- chain tool
- Allen wrenches
- needle-nose pliers
- crescent wrench
- screwdriver
- spare brake cable
- lubricant
- rag
- electrical tape

MAINTENANCE

How do you keep the steed running smoothly on road or trail? Both the constant rattle of trail riding and the extra weight of touring are hard on a bike: equipment fails more often and wears out more quickly. Each time you ride, check your bike over: make sure the brake pads strike the rims properly, check the headset, be sure the wheels are seated in the dropouts, and spin the pedals to test the action of the drivetrain.

While all bikes will eventually sink out of tune, mud haunts the mountain bike. Mud causes brakes to fail, derailleurs to stop functioning, bearings to grind square, and, worst, makes your bike look so ugly. Tourists have the same problem, to a lesser extent, with road grit. To fight against mud and grit you'll need to keep your bike clean. What's the best way to clean your bike off? Some

Last-minute maintenance

bike shops tell you to let the mud dry, then whisk the mud off with a heavy brush, so you won't taint your bike with water. In dry climates, this is a good way to clean your bike. But in wet climates, it's much too complicated and time-consuming. Bikes get drenched while riding and soaked while on top of the car, so it doesn't seem like a little more water will hurt. Go ahead, hose the thing down until the dirt is gone, then dry it off with a rag. When the bearings grind square, replace them. If you never clean your bike, at least lubricate your chain and then wipe the chain off with a rag before each ride.

As far as other bicycle maintenance goes, usually the bike will let you know when things aren't running smoothly. When it looks or feels as though something is not working so well, figure out what's wrong and fix it or take it in to a qualified mechanic. Remember: Every bike should run smoothly. The corollary: It's a lot less painful to extract a twenty from your wallet now than to stand on the trail in the rain, looking at a non-functioning bike.

Maintenance suggestions

- Always keep your chain clean and lubricated.
- Always keep the brake pad surface flat (file them down) and your brakes adjusted properly.
- Keep the wheels true.
- Replace your chain every 800 miles.
- Replace your freewheel when the teeth become hooked and asymmetrical.
- Replace thin tires, frayed cables, and cracked or worn rims.
- Repack bearings twice a year.
- Replace your socks daily.

TRAINING AND VICES

Everyone wants to be able to hop on the bike and ride for miles without fatigue. For many, though, a day of mountain biking or touring means an evening of zoning out and an early bedtime. It is possible to get into good enough shape so that you can enjoy the evening (or at least remember it). Two key points allow for bicycling with less fatigue. Riding skill is the first key. If you are a beginning rider, you expend lots of energy worrying, gripping the handle bars too tight, maneuvering around small obstacles, constantly starting and stopping, and probably pushing the wrong gears. The only advice I can give is to practice.

Obviously, being fit is the second element. Being in shape doesn't mean riding thousands of miles at top speed; it means molding your fitness so that you work on strength and endurance. If the endurance part is missing, you will bonk after an hour or two and your friends will abandon you because of your grumpiness; if the strength part is missing, your leg muscles will shred (the bad kind) on the first hard climb, and your friends will leave you because you are riding so slow. Start out with road rides or trail rides known to be easy, so you don't overdo it the first few times out. To improve endurance, ride on the flats for many hours with your pulse at or slightly above 130 beats per minute. You ought to be able to hold a conversation most of the way.

To gain strength, go on rides that emphasize hills and sprints. Try using larger gears on these rides. These rides should be varied; at times your pulse should reach 90 percent of your maximum (220 minus your age). At the top of each hill you should be gasping for breath, unable to utter a word. I recommend putting in at least a month of quality endurance riding before you begin any strength rides. Once you begin these strength rides, remember to continue to go on the longer endurance rides. And always remember to alternate between hard days and easy days. To stay in shape, you need to exercise at least four times each week, three of which should be bicycling. If you are planning a long tour, you should ride six days each week and emphasize the endurance rides over the strength rides.

VICES: Now that you are in shape, I'll try to wreck it by offering donuts and ropes of licorice. Junk food is the pirate of the food world, plundering our bodies with blank calories, heaps of sodium, and buckets of fat. Athletes like to argue that exercise mediates the downside of these rogue foods. Olympic marathon runner Don Kardong has said a million times that without ice cream there would be darkness and chaos in the world. My question is: What about hamburgers, chips, donuts, red wine, and bulk cookies?

Indeed, no rules regarding vices and mountain biking exist, although many a dogmatic bicyclist will lecture you differently. Plato, wise man that he was, urged us to search for a golden mean, a point between excesses. I suggest there is a golden mean between many vices and none.

VIRTUOUS CYCLING

According to Aristotle, mountain bikers cycle for one of three reasons: utility, pleasure, or virtue. The utility in mountain biking is working out, perfecting riding skills, learning about wild areas so they won't be abused. The pleasure in mountain biking is the thrill, the friendships, the beauty. But how can you be a virtuous mountain bicyclist? The virtuous mountain bicyclist gets a workout and perfects riding skills, revels in the friendships and tall trees, but the virtuous mountain biker also thinks beyond these immediate things and enters a spiritual world of what is best, what is *Good*.

The environment

Everyone who enters a primitive area must take responsibility to minimize his or her impact. Since the average mountain bike weighs about 30 pounds, a loaded hiker bounding down the trail outweighs a mountain bicyclist (horses are off the scale). These facts jibe with recently published scientific studies, includ-

Redwoods in northern California

ing the 1994 *Erosional Impact of Hikers, Horses, Motorcycles, and Off-Road Bicycles on Mountain Trails in Montana* by John Wilson and Joseph Seney (available from IMBA, see page 33), which show that bicycles and boots displace about the same amount of sediment, on dry and wet trails (again, horses are off the scale). In many instances, bicycle tires actually improve trail conditions by compacting the trail surface for future use. But a bicycle tire can also damage the trail in certain circumstances. First, mountain bikers should never lock up the brakes and skid on soft-surface trails. Bicyclists must learn how to descend and ride at low speeds or dismount and walk. This is critical on trails with switchbacks, which are especially sensitive to erosion. Second, on soft soils or on poorly constructed trails, a bicycle tire can form an impression in the trail surface which can channel water and erode the trail. Trail conditions can change quickly, so watch the trail for signs of damage. Walk your bike around delicate or muddy sections. It's up to each user—pedestrian, equestrian, cyclist—to survey his impact and then take action to prevent damage, *turning around if necessary*.

The greatest damage to trails comes not from wheels or boots but from overuse. Over the past twenty years, U.S. trail mileage has decreased while the population of trail users has grown: more folks are traversing each mile of trail. More well-built, multi-use trails are needed. But users need to take responsibility for the land and help disperse the use. If a trail is too crowded, then select another one next time. *This will thus minimize the most serious impact—overcrowding.*

Aesthetics

Hiking and equestrian groups have been exceptionally vocal in their opposition to mountain bikes, but it's an aesthetic issue, not a trail-use problem. User conflict and environmental damage are euphemisms for a not-on-my-trail attitude. These groups feel as though mountain bikers are infringing on their trails. "Their" trails happen to be located on public land.

Trail users venture into wild and beautiful areas to get away from the crowds, to be self-sufficient, to be out there. But as the population grows, finding this peace is more and more difficult, especially near urban areas. Of course it's still possible to find that isolated spot—users just might have to go farther to get there. The 6-billion-people-on-the-planet paradigm makes solitary trails close to cities harder to find. Trail users must learn to either expect to see others on the trail or spend more time searching out remote places. Unfortunately, some user groups choose to fight over crowded trails close to home rather than enjoying beautiful, solitary trails a little farther away. It's telling that most trail-use bickering is over trails close to urban areas. In Idaho, for instance, most trails outside of designated wilderness areas are multiple-use trails. What we need are more trails and a new attitude about trails close to urban areas; what we don't need are segregated trails.

Some have argued, spuriously, that mountain bicycles are a new use, and thus upset the proprietary grip hikers and equestrians hold on public trails. But while the term "mountain bicycle" is relatively new, hearty cyclists have been experiencing the beauty and wonder of remote areas on bicycles for over a century. In an article describing a Wyoming bicycle tour in an 1883 issue of *The Wheelman*, W.O. Owen writes, "All around us beautiful evergreens tossed in the wind, each one gorgeously attired in Nature's own drapery." Owen was out there for the same reason most mountain bikers are: for the wonderful experience of the wild. Indeed, the land-use argument between bicyclists, hikers, and equestrians is really just an intramural one. *All three groups want to save public land from destruction and keep it beautiful and wild into the future.*

The dispute over rights

Many trails and entire areas have been closed to mountain bicycles. Currently, mountain bikes are excluded from trails in all national parks and completely barred from designated wilderness areas. Many local jurisdictions have also restricted the use of bicycles in parks and green belts. Bicycles have been

Talking to a group of equestrians

banned from thousands of miles of perfectly suited multi-use trails.

As far as I can tell, the restrictions originated from a semantic problem: during the mountain bike boom of the last ten years, land managers didn't have a column in their manuals for mountain bicycles. Egged on by a small number of other trail users, managers banned bicycles because it seemed to be the easy way to go. Of course rarely did this have to do with science, empirical trail studies, or real user conflict. My experience has been that land managers who don't ride bicycles tend to close trails while managers who do enjoy the activity work to keep them open.

The reality is that miners, timber companies, horse use, recreational shooting, and vandalism have millions of times more impact on wild areas and beautiful trails than hikers or bicyclists, yet these activities continue on public lands that have been closed to mountain bicycles. Give me a break.

If the way you interact with public land adversely affects me, then either you shouldn't be doing it or you should pay me for the inconvenience. When users damage sensitive areas—and there can be no argument that motorcyclists, equestrians, and miners do—they should pay us (through restrictions and/or use fees based on the impact) for degrading our land. If hikers and bicyclists damage the trail, then they ought to pay as well, perhaps with annual licenses. But regulation and soapboxing only goes so far. All users need to make personal decisions about the way they interact with wild lands. *Keep in mind the pristine aesthetic we're all searching for and it will be Good.*

The rules

- Leave no trace: No Power Bar wrappers, treadmarks, toilet paper, or the clear plastic from the back of tube patches.
- Do not skid—ever. Mountain bikers should avoid riding after a heavy rain or anytime the ground is unstable and liable to be marred. Walk around delicate areas.
- Respect all other trail users. Yield the right of way to everyone, including hikers, runners, other bicyclists, motorcyclists, and equestrians.
- Stop and dismount when you encounter equestrians. Stand on the downhill side of the trail, and talk to the horse and rider as they pass.
- Ride in control.
- Respect wildlife.
- Never shred around corners at 50 miles per hour screaming "Mountain biker from hell!"

GETTING INVOLVED

If you are interested in land issues and want to help educate land managers, legislators, and the media about mountain bicycling, call or write them. Tell them which trails you enjoy and why, and then tell them you are a bicyclist and an environmentalist. It's not an oxymoron. Most activism takes place at the local level. The publications, organizations, and agencies listed below are a good place to start; a call to the local club or county park office could help even more.

Publications

Northwest Cyclist	206-286-8566
The Bicycle Paper (Seattle, WA)	206-323-3301
Oregon Cycling	503-686-9885
California Bicyclist	415-546-7291

Bicycling clubs

Cycling British Columbia	604-737-3034
Backcountry Bicycle Trail Club (Seattle, WA)	206-283-2995
Cascade Bicycle Club (Seattle, WA)	206-522-2453
Portland United Mountain Pedalers (Portland, OR)	503-223-3954
Bicycle Trails Council of Marin (Marin County, CA)	415-456-7512
Responsible Organized Mountain Pedalers (Campbell, CA)	408-534-1130
International Mountain Bike Association (IMBA)	303-545-9011
National Off-Road Bicycle Association	719-578-4717

Jurisdictions

British Columbia Provincial Parks	604-924-2200
Washington State Parks	206-902-8563
Oregon State Parks	503-378-6305
California State Parks	916-653-6995
National Forest Service: Pacific Northwest Region	503-326-2954
National Forest Service: Pacific Southwest Region	415-705-2874

BRITISH COLUMBIA
& WASHINGTON

PRELUDE

I don't know if I've ever been as cold as the day in November I went mountain biking on Mount Constitution (see page 47). I had the proper gear—gloves, jersey and jacket, long underwear, riding pants, a wool hat—but there I was, up on the top of the mountain next to the stone tower, trying to fend off the insistent shaking.

The long ride up from our camp at Moran State Park had been pleasant. The beautiful day and steady climb had even convinced me to take off my jacket. At the top, I put my jacket back on and climbed up the tower. The view was incredible, north to the Canadian Gulf Islands, south to Mount Rainier, west to the Strait of Juan de Fuca. If my eyes were just adjusted properly, it seemed possible to see from Whistler, B.C., all the way south to Santa Barbara, Calif. Hardly a day to worry about getting cold.

From the southern edge of the mountain, near the single-track trail we would soon descend, we looked down at Twin Lakes—our destination. Using a current of wind, a bald eagle rounded the corner of the mountain and glided slowly by, then circled over the lakes 1,500 ft. below.

I began to notice the shaking then, kind of a shiver that wouldn't go away, an uncomfortable ice-block feeling in my toes. But instead of quickly leaving, we watched the eagle loop and loop above the lakes. When we finally did begin riding, I could hardly pedal, none of my muscles seemed to work. The smallest bump in the trail proved impossible; the braking on this epic downhill, futile. I chastised myself for bike touring so late in the year, for lingering too long at the top, for not bringing twice as much gear (although it would have been difficult to wear many more layers). Why had I selected the San Juan Islands—with the ferries and winter storms—rather than some sunny California stretch of road? At a stop, a friend showed me how to windmill my arms to force blood back into my hands. Five minutes later I was freezing again.

Yet when I think back on it, I don't remember the cold as much as I do that eagle soaring above the lakes and the small white tracks the ferries made in the dark water.

TOUR GUIDE

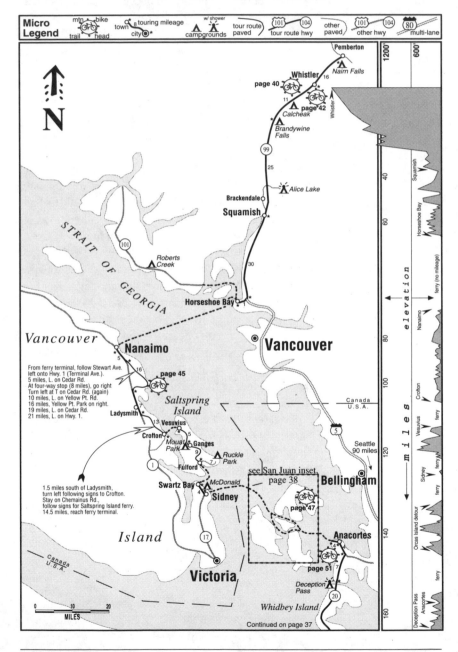

Micro Legend: mtn trail, bike head, town, city, touring mileage, w/ shower campgrounds, tour route paved, tour route hwy 101/104, other paved 101/104, other hwy, 80 multi-lane

N

Pemberton

Nairn Falls

Whistler 16

page 40

page 42
Calcheak

Brandywine Falls

99

25

Alice Lake

Brackendale

Squamish

STRAIT

101

Roberts Creek

OF

30

GEORGIA

Horseshoe Bay

Vancouver

Nanaimo

Vancouver

From ferry terminal, follow Stewart Ave.
left onto Hwy. 1 (Terminal Ave.).
5 miles, L. on Cedar Rd.
At four-way stop (8 miles), go right
Turn left at T on Cedar Rd. (again)
10 miles, L. on Yellow Pt. Rd.
16 miles, Yellow Pt. Park on right.
19 miles, L. on Cedar Rd.
21 miles, L. on Hwy. 1.

page 45

Saltspring Island

Canada U.S.A.

Ladysmith

5

Seattle 90 miles

Vesuvius

13

Crofton

Mouat Park

Ganges

9

Ruckle Park

1

Fulford

1.5 miles south of Ladysmith,
turn left following signs to Crofton.
Stay on Chemainus Rd.,
follow signs for Saltspring Island ferry.
14.5 miles, reach ferry terminal.

Swartz Bay

McDonald

see San Juan inset, page 38

Bellingham

Sidney

4

page 47

Island

17

Anacortes

Canada U.S.A.

page 51

Victoria

Deception Pass

20

0   10   20
MILES

Whidbey Island

Continued on page 37

elevation   miles

1200' 600'

40 60 80 100 120 140 160

Squamish, Horseshoe Bay, Nanaimo, Crofton, Vesuvius, Sidney, Orcas Island detour, Deception Pass, Anacortes

ferry (no mileage)

TOUR GUIDE

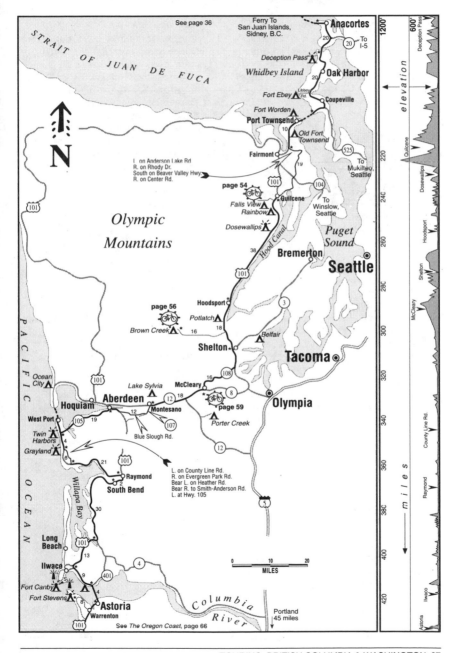

QUICK FACTS

miles (touring south from Whistler, B.C.)

0   **SLEEP**: To start off the tour with a roof over your head, a hot breakfast, and a hot tub, you couldn't ask for more than **Chalet Luise** ☎ 604-932-4187, located near Whistler Village. Luise and Eric—mountain bikers themselves—run a

crispy clean, moderately priced pension in the best Swiss style. Bikes in the garage; reservations advised.

0   **EAT:** For a Greek dinner with the chef from Olympus, try **Zeuski's**. Located in Whistler Village, this seems to be the locals' choice due to the good food, inexpensive wine, and late hours.

0   **READ:** *Whistler Off-Road Cycling Guide*, by Charlie Doyle and Grant Lamont. Everybody uses this little mountain bike guide. One caution: the ride descriptions are short. How short? Sometimes short on important details.

0   **REPAIR:** Beyond the two rides in *Wild Pigs*, pages 40 and 42, plenty of bikable trails criss-cross the mountains surrounding Whistler. More information can be gleaned at **Mountain Riders** ☎ 604-932-3659 or **Whistler Backroads** ☎ 604-932-3111.

1   **EAT:** If you're not staying at a B&B, the funky **Southside Deli** (2102 Lake Placid Rd.) casually prepares great breakfasts, including the King Kong Kake, a pancake so big it requires a forklift to serve.

41   **EAT & SEE:** For those who appreciate bizarre juxtapositions, enjoy tea and cinnamon bun at **Jane's Coffeehouse** while gazing across a gravel parking area at dinosaur-sized dump trucks and the seven-story "concentration" building of the **British Columbia Museum of Mining**.

67   **SLEEP:** Due to the dearth of camping between Whistler and Saltspring Is-

miles (touring south from Whistler, B.C.)

land, try **Horseshoe Bay Motel** before catching the ferry ☎ 604-921-7454. For more beds over the next 50 touring miles, call the **Gulf Islands B&B Reservation Service** ☎ 604-539-5390. They track rooms for over 100 B&Bs.

67   **EAT:** Pastries can be found in Horseshoe Bay at **Hammonds Deli** (6611 Royal Ave.), close to the ferry terminal.

85   **CAMP: Campgrounds in the Gulf Islands** may be closed off-season. Call ahead ☎ 604-391-2300.

135   **INFO:** If you plan to drive in the Gulf or San Juan Islands: First, ferries fill up quickly in

the summer (get in line early); second, ferries cost much more if you use a roof rack for your bike. **Gulf Island Ferries** ☎ 604-629-3215. **Washington State Ferries** ☎ 206-464-6400.

135   **REPAIR: Dolphin Bay Bicycles** on Orcas ☎ 360-376-4157.

145   **INSET:** San Juan Islands.

From ferry terminal, follow the arterial—the Horseshoe Hwy.—past Eastsound to Moran State Park and Cascade Lake.

To Sidney, B.C.

Point Doughty

Orcas ▲ Eastsound *Island*

12

Mountain ▲Lake

8

Doe Bay

Orcas

Roche Harbor

Shaw I.

Cascade Lake

Friday Harbor

San Juan Island

Spencer Spit

To Anacortes

Lopez Island

145 **SEE & CAMP:** If you've got the energy to cycle up **Mount Constitution**, on clear days you'll be rewarded with a spectacular view of the San Juan Islands and the mountains beyond. Camping at **Moran State Park** is tight, though recommended, so call for availability ☎ 360-376-2326.

145* **SLEEP:** For a bit more rustic adventuring, check out tie-dyed **Doe Bay** ☎ 360-376-2291 on Orcas Island. Although not a B&B, you do get your

choice of cabin, camping, or tree house. Bike tourists on the down and out may be able to work for meals in the cafe. Impromptu volleyball games, sea kayak lessons, and long soaks in the hot tubs may get you behind schedule on your Pacific coast tour.

158 **READ:** The city of Anacortes publishes two excellent trail maps: *Trail Guide to the Anacortes Community Forest Lands* (see page 51).

165 **CAMP:** One of the most idyllic camp-

grounds on the coast, **Deception Pass** holds a balance between the rushing currents and sheer cliffs of the nearby strait—Deception Pass—and the peaceful, chameleon-like Cranberry Lake. One of the most popular campgrounds in Washington State.

185 **REPAIR:** It's fun to walk through the historic district of Port Townsend. While there, stop by **P.T. Cyclery** at 100 Tyler ☎ 360-385-6470. They have the scoop on local mountain biking.

240* **SLEEP:** Across Puget Sound from Seattle, Bainbridge Island is off the touring route, but it's a wonderful place to rest if you happen to be checking out the Seattle mountain bike scene. **The**

Bombay House ☎ 206-842-3926 serves excellent breakfasts by Bunny, who authored a cookbook. Lucky guests may arrive in time for the occasional psychic readings. Bikes in the garage.

240* **READ:** If you are exploring the Seattle mountain bike scene: *Kissing the Trail: Greater Seattle Mountain Bicycle Adventures*, by John Zilly; *Mountain Bike Adventures in Washington's South Cascades* and *Mountain Bike Adventures in Washington's North Cascades*, both by Tom Kirkendall.

300 **REPAIR: Jerry's Ride and Slide**, Bike repair ☎ 360-495-3703 in McCleary.

425 **SLEEP:** Originally a Presbyterian Church, the **Chickadee Inn**, located in the feisty fishing village of Ilwaco ☎ 360-642-8686, provides a sense of spiritualness with an Agatha Christie edge. Nine cozy rooms on the second floor; a place for bikes in the basement.

425 **SLEEP:** Perhaps you will be blessed with the good luck of a constant tail wind if you stay at **Boreas** ☎ 360-642-8069, which means God of the north wind. This B&B, located in Long Beach (the ninth circle of kite flying), looks out over grasses to the Pacific Ocean. Play musical instruments with other guests or use the shed for minor bike repairs.

425 **SLEEP:** Everything booked? Try the **Long Beach B&B Association** ☎ 360-642-8484.

425 **CAMP & SEE:** Fort Canby rates as a second tier campground due to the procession of RVs in this busy, 250-site park. But to put your adventure in proper perspective, the **Lewis and Clark Interpretive Center** and the **Cape Disappointment Lighthouse**—both Ft. Canby sights, are highly recommended.

*indicates site off tour route

THE VALLEY TRAIL ✺

Checklist: 7.4 miles, Loop; dirt trail, paved trail
Duration: 1–2 hours
Hill factor: easy ups and downs, mostly flat
Skill level: beginner
Map: *Whistler Valley Directory map*
Season: summer, early fall
User density: high; cyclists, walkers, wheelchairs, roller bladers
Explorability: moderate

Teaser

The Valley Trail, easy and paved about half the way, provides a tour of Whistler. See beautiful mountain views as the trail makes a circuit of the valley, passing from park to park, along the River of Golden Dreams, and then through Whistler Village (or, more accurately, Whistler shopping and eating). If you are a shopper and get stuck passing your VISA around in the Village, expect this loop to take significantly more time.

Ride

Beginning at Dream River Park follow the signs for the Valley Trail—ride out a gravelly road. **Whoa,** throughout this ride trails exit from the main trail. Be certain to stay on the main trail, following the Valley Trail signs. Begin climbing just before the **1 mile** point. The road ascends steadily for about one-half mile, then undulates up and down until reaching Lost Lake Beach at **2.4 miles**. From the beach, follow the signs toward Whistler Village.

At **3.7 miles**, the pavement begins near the Village. From here the official trail is difficult to trace as it winds through the Whistler shopping area, but at **4.2 miles** you should be crossing Highway 99 and finding the Valley Trail on the opposite side. When the trail divides, take the right fork, following the signs toward Meadow Park. The paved trail winds past a golf course and numerous condominiums. Along the way, the trail forks several more times; each time follow the signs for Meadow Park.

At **7 miles**, reach Meadow Park. Continue on the Valley Trail to Highway 99 at **7.3 miles**. Cross the highway and complete the loop at Dream River Park, at **7.4 miles**.

VALLEY TRAIL

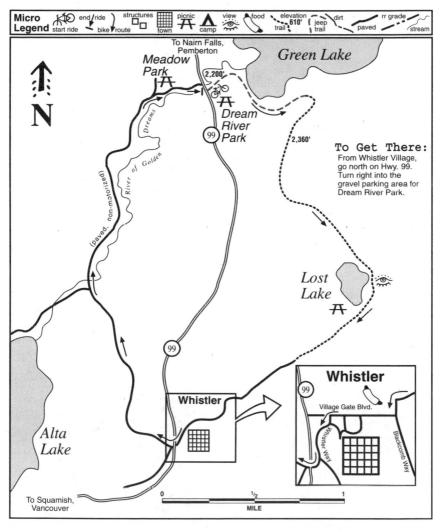

Micro Legend
end/ride | start ride | bike/route | structures | picnic/town | camp | view | food | elevation 610' trail | jeep trail | dirt | rr grade | paved | stream

To Nairn Falls, Pemberton

Green Lake

Meadow Park

2,200'

Dream River Park

99

2,360'

River of Golden Dreams

(paved, non-motorized)

To Get There:
From Whistler Village, go north on Hwy. 99. Turn right into the gravel parking area for Dream River Park.

Lost Lake

Whistler

99

Village Gate Blvd.

Whistler Way

Blackcomb Way

Alta Lake

99

Whistler

To Squamish, Vancouver

0   1/2   1
MILE

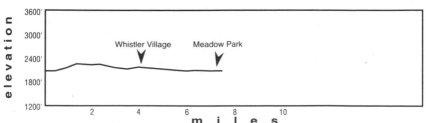

elevation

3600'
3000'
2400'
1800'
1200'

Whistler Village   Meadow Park

2   4   6   8   10
m i l e s

BRANDYWINE FALLS ⊛⊛

Checklist: 10.5 miles, One Way; dirt trail, dirt road, highway
Duration: 2–3 hours
Hill factor: moderate ups and downs
Skill level: intermediate
Season: summer, fall
User density: low; cyclists, walkers, vehicles on parts
Explorability: moderate

Teaser

More accurately called the *way* to Brandywine Falls rather than the *trail* to Brandywine Falls, this ride patches together an odd series of trails and roads and railroad-track crossings before ending at the falls. It begins at a train station, crosses a beautiful river, winds through the city dump, rollercoasters along some cross-county ski trails, and ends up at a majestic waterfall so tall that it's difficult to fit it into a photograph. Pay attention and have a good attitude while route finding. Watch out for trucks at the dump.

Descending to the Cheakamus River near Whistler, British Columbia

Brandywine Falls

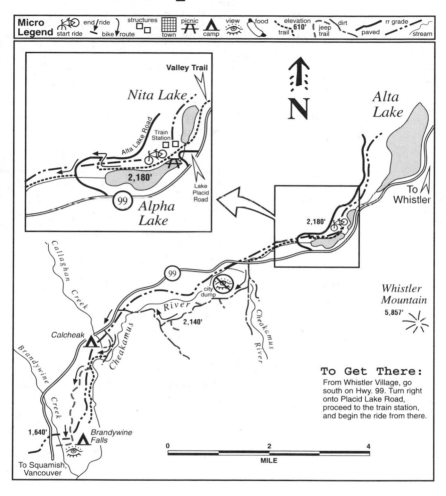

Micro Legend — end/ride, start ride, bike/route, structures, town, picnic, camp, view, food, elevation 610' trail, jeep trail, dirt, paved, rr grade, stream

N

Valley Trail

Nita Lake

Alta Lake Road

Train Station

2,180'

Alpha Lake

Lake Placid Road

99

Alta Lake

To Whistler

Callaghan Creek

99

city dump

Cheakamus River

2,140'

Cheakamus River

Calcheak

Brandywine Creek

1,640'

Brandywine Falls

To Squamish, Vancouver

2,180'

Whistler Mountain 5,857'

To Get There:

From Whistler Village, go south on Hwy. 99. Turn right onto Placid Lake Road, proceed to the train station, and begin the ride from there.

0   2   4
MILE

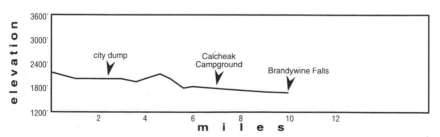

elevation: 3600', 3000', 2400', 1800', 1200'

city dump

Calcheak Campground

Brandywine Falls

miles: 2, 4, 6, 8, 10, 12

Ride

Beginning at the train station at Alpha Lake Park, ride southwest away from Whistler. (You can also begin this ride at Whistler Village via the Valley Trail.) The trail turns to dirt, running between the lake shore and the railroad tracks. Stay on the main road. At the end of Alpha Lake, cross the railroad tracks and climb the dirt hill on the right. Turn left onto Alpha Lake Road. Just after the second railroad crossing, turn right onto a gravelly trail.

At **2 miles**, cross Highway 99 to the dirt road on the opposite side. The road quickly crosses the wild Cheakamus River. Take the next right, following the signs toward the city dump. Arrive at the city dump, **2.5 miles**. **Whoa**, watch for trucks. Stay to the left of the landfill. At **3 miles** turn right, following the sign toward Brandywine Falls. Take the not-so-intuitive left fork at **3.75 miles**. After that, though, take the next two right turns as the road descends back toward the Cheakamus River. A bridge spans the river at **5.8 miles**. At **6.6 miles**, cross the railroad tracks to reach Highway 99. Turn left and pedal down the highway, but only for a short distance.

At **7 miles**, turn left onto a dirt road, crossing the railroad tracks again. Take the second right on the way to the Calcheak Campground. Then take the second right into the south part of the campground. Find the "trail" sign at **7.6 miles**. Immediately cross a suspension bridge across Callaghan Creek. Follow the single-track trail to a fork. **Whoa**, this is easy to miss. Take the right fork which crosses the railroad tracks and becomes a dirt road (don't take the trail). Turn left onto a jeep trail under some power lines. From here the road, which doubles as a cross-country ski track in winter, rollercoasters down to Brandywine Falls at **10.5 miles**.

YELLOW POINT PARK ✿✿✿

Checklist: 1.7 miles, Loop; dirt trail
Duration: 1 hour or less
Hill factor: easy ups and downs
Skill level: advanced
Map: wooden sign with map at trail entrance
Season: spring, summer, fall
User density: moderate; cyclists, walkers
Explorability: moderate

Teaser

The Yellow Point Park ride, the shortest in this book at just under two miles, gives the wandering tourist a chance to get into the woods for a short stretch before hitting the road again. A pleasant spot for a picnic, this small provincial park has approximately four more miles of single-track trails. Although the terrain is quite level, pushing may be necessary in places due to the sometimes narrow and technical trails.

Winding through Yellow Point Park on Vancouver Island

YELLOW POINT PARK

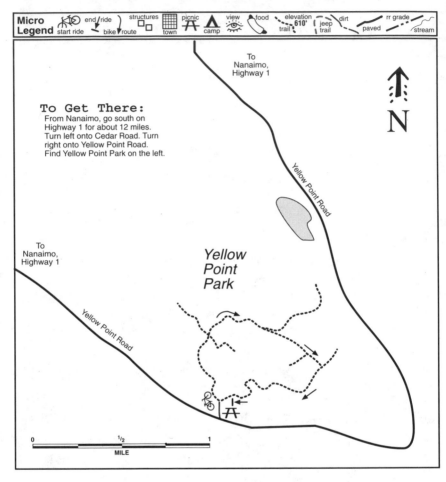

Micro Legend — start ride, end ride, bike route, structures, town, picnic, camp, view, food, elevation 610', trail, jeep trail, dirt, paved, rr grade, stream

To Get There:
From Nanaimo, go south on Highway 1 for about 12 miles. Turn left onto Cedar Road. Turn right onto Yellow Point Road. Find Yellow Point Park on the left.

To Nanaimo, Highway 1

Yellow Point Road

Yellow Point Park

To Nanaimo, Highway 1

Yellow Point Road

N

0   ½   1
MILE

Ride

From the parking lot take the trail on the left near the trail map sign. At **.3 mile**, follow the signs that point to the Main Trail. Immediately reach a 4-way intersection. Lesser trails go right and left. Stay on the Main Trail, straight, as it drops down the hill. Moderately technical single track through the woods. Lots of lesser trails spur off, but stay on the Main Trail by following signs. At **.4 mile**, cross a short bridge over a muddy area. The trail forks immediately after the bridge but rejoins itself shortly—either route works.

Then at **.5 mile**, the trail forks—turn right. Find another fork at **.6 mile**—take the narrower left route (basically straight). At **.8 mile**, come to a T and turn right. The trail returns to the parking area at **1.7 miles**.

MORAN STATE PARK ✿✿✿✿

Checklist: 15.1 miles, Loop; paved road, dirt trail,
Duration: 3–5 hours
Hill factor: long, difficult climb at beginning
Skill level: advanced
Map: *Moran State Park map*
Season: fall/spring—**WHOA**, closed between May 15 and Sept. 15
User density: moderate; cyclists, hikers
Explorability: moderate

Teaser

This is an incredible ride, spiraling to the top of Mount Constitution (2,610 ft.) on the road and then single tracking it back down through the layers of ecosystems. From the top of the mountain, wave patterns on Puget Sound seem to stand still, and you can see Mount Baker, Glacier Peak, Mount Rainier, and Mount Olympus by just turning in a circle. This trail is closed to bicycles during the busy summer season between May 15 and September 15. Do not ride during these times or the park may be closed to bicycles year round. During the off season, it can get cold, so be careful of hypothermia. After climbing over 2610 ft. and sweating most of the way, the chill at the top can come fast and hard.

Climbing Mount Constitution, Orcas Island

MORAN STATE PARK

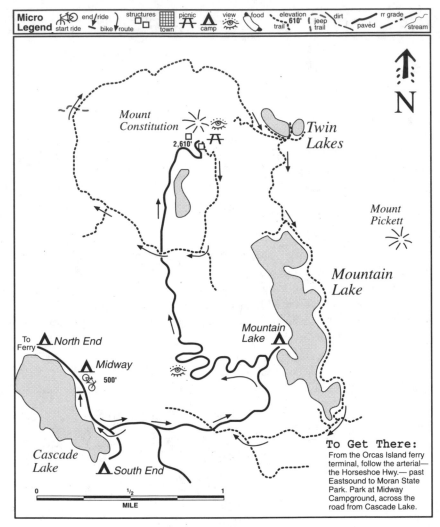

Micro Legend — end/ride, start ride, bike route, structures, town, picnic, camp, view, food, elevation 610', trail, jeep trail, dirt, paved, rr grade, stream

Mount Constitution
2,610'

Twin Lakes

Mount Pickett

Mountain Lake

Mountain Lake

To Ferry

North End

Midway
500'

Cascade Lake

South End

0   ½   1
MILE

To Get There:
From the Orcas Island ferry terminal, follow the arterial— the Horseshoe Hwy.— past Eastsound to Moran State Park. Park at Midway Campground, across the road from Cascade Lake.

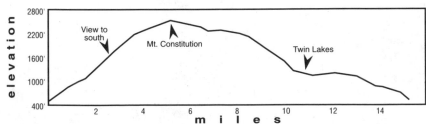

Resting at the top of Mount Constitution, Orcas Island

Ride

From the parking area at the Midway Campground, pedal south up the paved road that borders Cascade Lake. At **.5 mile**, take the left fork up towards Mount Constitution. At **.9 mile** pass a trailhead on right and left—continue up the road. The way becomes steep and relentless for the next three miles. Cross a bridge at **1.3 miles**. When the road forks at **1.6 miles**, take the left fork following the signs up to Mount Constitution. (The right fork goes to the small, wonderful Mountain Lake Campground). Pass a spectacular southward lookout after a long slog, **2.7 miles**. At **3.6 miles**, the road flattens a bit. At **4.2 miles**, there's a trailhead on either side—continue up the road. At **5.2 miles**, reach the parking lot at the top. The tower and lookout are 70 yards up the dirt road.

From the stone tower, find the trail to the south, **5.4 miles**, that drops behind the bathrooms and then away from the parking lot. The single-track trail drops and traverses through sparse pine forest. At **6.4 miles** reach an intersection—turn right toward Cold Springs. Upon arriving at the road to the top of the mountain at **6.7 miles**, cross it and find trail on the other side. The trail forks at **7.3 miles**, take the right fork toward Twin Lakes. At **8.4 miles**, cross a primitive road to the trail on other side.

At **10.1 miles**, reach a T in the trail. (Right heads back up Mount Constitution.) Turn left and ride quickly down to Twin Lakes. At **10.4 miles**, reach the first lake in the twin chain and a 4-way intersection. A hard left swings around the lake. A left splits Twin Lakes and then climbs up around Picket Mountain (this ride is longer and more difficult). Instead, take the right and ride toward Mountain Lake Landing. Confront another fork at **11.1 miles**. At this point, you must turn left because bikes are not allowed on the west side of Mountain Lake.

From here the trail becomes more technical as it winds around the east side of the lake. There are several short climbs. When the trail meets a jeep trail at a T at **13 miles**, turn right. (Left takes you toward Mount Picket.) Pass the dam at the end of the lake, drop to the left, and then when the trail forks, go left, continuing downhill.

At **13.8 miles**, the trail arrives at a T—turn right onto the jeep trail. (Just past a bridge and a tiny waterfall.) Find a fork at **14 miles**—stay on the jeep trail, right. At **14.2 miles**, reach a dirt parking lot and the paved Mount Constitution road. At the road, turn left and ride downhill to the Midway Campground to complete the ride, **15.1 miles**.

Gliding toward Twin Lakes, Moran State Park

CRANBERRY LAKE ✿✿✿

Checklist: 11.1 miles, Loop; dirt trail
Duration: 2–3 hours
Hill factor: rolling
Skill level: intermediate
Map: *Cranberry Lake*, Anacortes Community Forest Lands
Season: spring, summer, fall
User density: moderate; cyclists, hikers, equestrians
Explorability: high

Teaser

The city of Anacortes did a farsighted thing when they bought and set aside the Anacortes Community Forest Lands, much like Arcata, California (see page 107). To their credit, most of the trails are open to all users. The trails through the second-growth forests provide beautiful (except for the excursion past the old city dump), terrific riding for all abilities.

Waiting at Cranberry Lake for the riders to return

CRANBERRY LAKE

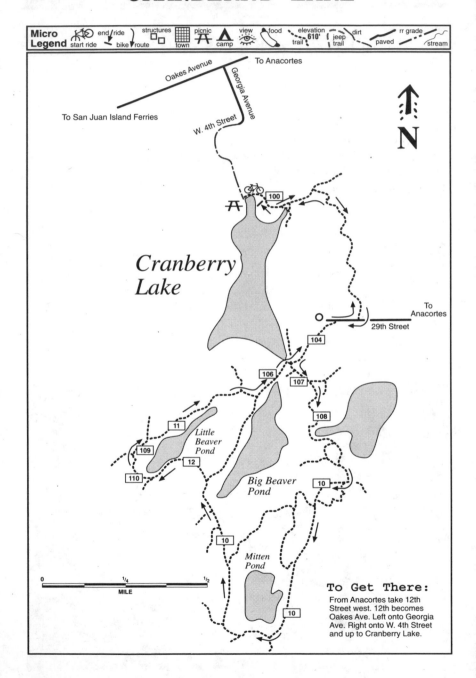

Micro Legend — end/ride, start ride, bike route, structures, town, picnic, camp, view, food, elevation 610' trail, jeep trail, dirt, paved, rr grade, stream

N

Oakes Avenue

To Anacortes

Georgia Avenue

To San Juan Island Ferries

W. 4th Street

100

Cranberry Lake

To Anacortes
29th Street

104

106

107

108

11

Little Beaver Pond

109

110

12

Big Beaver Pond

10

10

Mitten Pond

10

0   1/4   1/2
MILE

To Get There:
From Anacortes take 12th Street west. 12th becomes Oakes Ave. Left onto Georgia Ave. Right onto W. 4th Street and up to Cranberry Lake.

Ride

From the parking area at the north end of the Cranberry Lake, take the trail that crosses the spillway, east. The trail, narrow with occasional roots, climbs away from the lake. (The trails along the lake are off limits to bicycles.) After **.1 mile** the trail divides: take the left fork.

At **.5 mile** reach another fork and this time go right. Take the right fork again at **.7 mile**, riding along a winding, rooted trail. At **1.15 miles**, reach a paved road and turn right, climbing the hill toward a green water tank. Just after the road becomes gravel, find a trail on your left, **1.3 miles**.

At **1.5 miles**, reach a four-way intersection. Turn left, and then, when the trail divides again in twenty yards, take a second left onto Trail #108a. At **1.6 miles**, the trail forks yet again: turn right. At **1.75 miles**, reach the intersection of #108b and #108a, and stay to the left. After crossing several bridges, take the left trail at **1.95 miles**. Then ignore the small trail to the left at **2.0 miles**. Ten yards farther reach a dirt road which is Trail #10.

Turn right upon reaching Trail #10. The road bends slowly to the left as it passes the old city dump and then becomes a wide trail past a gate, **2.2 miles**. From here to the **8.5-mile mark**, pass numerous trails on the right and left, each time remaining on the well-used Trail #10.

Reach a fork at **8.5 miles** and take a left onto Trail #12. Ride along Little Beaver Pond to a fork at **8.8 miles**. Exit Trail #12—which goes left—and take Trail #110 to the right. At **8.9 miles**, Trail #110 T's at Trail #109: turn right onto Trail #109.

These trails, #110 and #109, are more technical—narrow and winding—than the wider trails #10, #11, and #12. Trail #109 becomes Trail #11, then at **9.3 miles** reach the intersection of Trail #11 and Trail #105. Turn right.

At **9.4 miles**, take a left onto Trail #10. After thirty yards, turn left again onto Trail #106. At **9.5 miles**, reach Cranberry Lake. Cross the little wooden bridge. A trail bends around the lake to the left, but it's off limits to bikes. Instead, cross the bridge and immediately turn right up a steep bank—you'll have to walk this short section. At **9.6 miles**, the loop has been returned to the four-way intersection. From the intersection retrace steps to the spillway at the north end of Cranberry Lake.

The retrace goes like this: straight through the intersection, taking Trail #104 to the green water tank and the road, **9.8 miles**. From the road turn left onto Trail #104. Following Trail #104, take two lefts and a right before reaching the parking area at **11.1 miles**.

LOWER BIG QUILCENE ✦✦✦

Checklist: 13 miles, Out & Back; dirt trail
Duration: 3–5 hours
Hill factor: rolling, then steady climbing
Skill level: intermediate
Map: *Tyler Peak*, *Mount Walker*, USGS
Season: spring, summer, fall
User density: high; cyclists, hikers, equestrians
Explorability: low

Teaser

Known as the Lower Big Quil to Olympic Peninsula locals, this is one of the best intermediate rides on the coast. The ultimately ridable trail, a smooth, well-maintained single track, rolls along the side of a ridge above the Big Quilcene River. After dropping down to the river and crossing it twice, the way follows the

river, through old, dark forests. At the end of the trail, either turn around and retrace your steps, or take Forest Service Rd. 2750 and 27 back to the trailhead. Taking the road makes the ride an 18.5-mile Loop rather than a 13-mile Out & Back.

Ride

From the trailhead of Trail #833, ride north. The way drops for a mile, then gradually climbs. The rollercoasters and well-maintained tread make for quick riding. However, try to keep the speed moderate, so other trail users can also enjoy this popular trail.

At **2 miles**, cross the Big Quilcene River. At **2.8 miles**, pass Bark Shanty Camp on the right. A

LOWER BIG QUILECENE

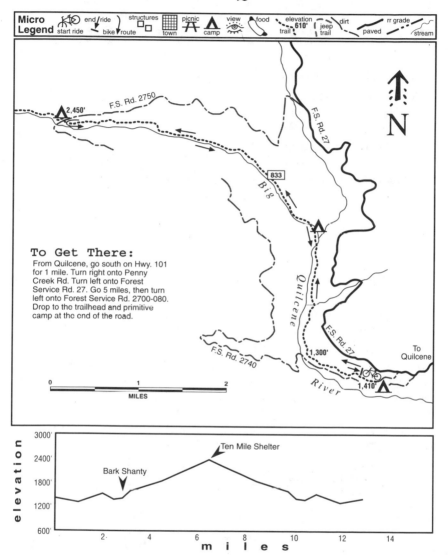

Micro Legend: start ride, end ride, bike route, structures, town, picnic, camp, view, food, elevation 610' trail, jeep trail, dirt, paved, rr grade, stream

F.S. Rd. 2750

2,450'

F.S. Rd. 27

833

Big

Quilcene

To Get There:
From Quilcene, go south on Hwy. 101 for 1 mile. Turn right onto Penny Creek Rd. Turn left onto Forest Service Rd. 27. Go 5 miles, then turn left onto Forest Service Rd. 2700-080. Drop to the trailhead and primitive camp at the end of the road.

F.S. Rd. 2740

F.S. Rd. 27

1,300'

River

1,410'

To Quilcene

N

0   1   2
MILES

Ten Mile Shelter

Bark Shanty

elevation: 3000', 2400', 1800', 1200', 600'
miles: 2, 4, 6, 8, 10, 12, 14

tenth of a mile further, at **2.9 miles**, cross the river again.

From the second river crossing, the trail becomes more technical and the climb steadier. Pass Camp Jolley at **5 miles**. The trail turns steeper yet over the final mile and a half to Ten Mile Shelter, **6.5 miles**. Turn around here—Ten Mile Shelter stands at the edge of the Buckhorn Wilderness—and glide back to the trailhead.

SOUTH FORK SKOKOMISH ✿✿✿

Checklist: 10 miles, Out & Back; dirt trail
Duration: 3–4 hours
Hill factor: one steep climb
Skill level: intermediate
Map: *Mount Tebo*, USGS
Season: spring, summer, fall
User density: moderate; cyclists, hikers, equestrians
Explorability: low

Teaser

As a public service, the Forest Service hands out maps with trail descriptions for many popular trails. Unfortunately, the information provided has nothing to do with the actual trail. Example: the Lower South Fork of the Skokomish Trail, #873. For mountain bikes, the Forest Service rates this trail "easiest"; their elevation chart shows a gradual rise over the entire 11-mile route. The actual trail gains over 300 ft. over the first one-half mile, and the upriver sections of the trail can hardly be described as "easy." Unless you desire an epic, 8-hour ride, I recommend turning around at the 5-mile point. Don't let this discourage you, though: this is a beautiful ride, through ancient forests and moss-covered alder along the South Fork of the Skokomish River. Other than the first mile, which will require some walking, this is a pleasant, intermediate ride.

Photo by David Graves

Exploring a grove of old growth near the Skokomish River

SOUTH FORK SKOKOMISH

Micro Legend — end/ride • start ride • structures • bike/route • town • picnic • camp • view • food • elevation 610' • trail • jeep trail • dirt • paved • rr grade • stream

Mount Tebo

Olympic

National

Forest

To Camp Harps, access to F.S. Rd. 2361

880'

South Fork Skokomish River

F.S. Rd. 2361

Forest Service Rd. 23

F.S. Rd. 2353

873

960' 580'

Brown Creek Campground

To Get There:

From Highway 101 about halfway between Hoodsport and Shelton, take Valley Road west. At five miles, turn right onto Forest Service Road 23. Travel nine miles to Forest Service Road 2353, and turn right. Cross the river, take the next left, and find the trailhead on the left.

F.S. Rd. 23

0   1   2
MILES

To Valley Road, Highway 101

elevation: 2400' 1800' 1200' 600' 0'

miles: 2 4 6 8 10 12 14

Along the Skokomish River

Ride

From the bridge across the South Fork of the Skokomish River, turn left (Brown Creek Campground to the right) and travel less than one-quarter mile to the trailhead of Trail #873 on the left.

The trail immediately begins an extreme climb, switchbacking several times to the top at **.4 mile**. To save your legs, it is prudent to walk sections of this initial hill, especially if you haven't warmed up. At the top, find a fork—stay to the left.

From the top of the ridge, the trail switchbacks precipitously down toward the river. With the first hectic mile complete, the trail mellows, winding through old growth on a wide, well-maintained trail. The trail follows close to the river at times, through the gravelly flood plain; other sections wind away from the river past enormous cedar and the obvious signs of black-tailed deer and elk.

The trail becomes more technical, rocky, narrow, and rolling. At the **5-mile point**, the trail swings alongside the river, the perfect spot for a picnic or a quiet rumination about the Skokomish Watershed. Turn around here and ride back to the trailhead, **10 miles**.

Alternative

The super-adventurous rider can choose from several other options. Continuing upriver from the **5-mile point**, find a "horse ford" across the South Fork at **8.5 miles**. Ford the river here and ride back on Forest Service Road #2361 and #23, returning to the parking area at **19 miles**. **Whoa**, these roads have been washed out in a number of places and bike portages are required. The other option is to turn around and ride back to the parking area, making the ride **17 miles**. Both options are difficult, mandating good stamina and advanced riding skills.

LARCH MOUNTAIN ✿ ✿ ✿ ✿

Checklist: 21.9 miles, Loop; dirt trails, dirt roads
Duration: 4–6 hours
Hill factor: steady climb at start, then hard rolling
Skill level: advanced
Map: *Capitol State Forest*, Washington State DNR
Season: spring, summer, fall
User density: moderate; cyclists, hikers, ORVs
Explorability: high

Teaser

The Washington State Department of Natural Resources maintains Capitol Forest, an immense forested area bounded by Interstate 5, Highway 12, and Highway 8. Literally hundreds of miles of trails and logging roads criss-cross the forest, providing an overwhelming selection of mountain bike possibilities. The trails in Capitol Forest range from smooth, well-maintained thoroughfares to rocky stream beds to mud bogs masquerading as trails. Generally, the trails in the motorized, north half of the forest are in better condition, though during the dry months—July and August—it probably makes no difference. The Larch Moun-

*Dirt road in
Capitol Forest*

LARCH MOUNTAIN

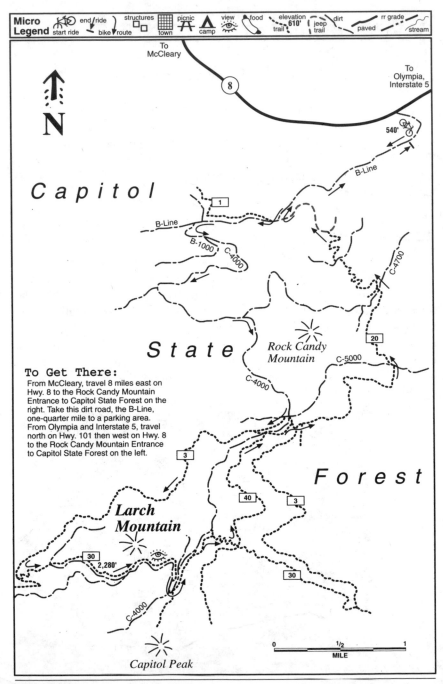

Micro Legend — end/ride · start ride · bike route · structures · town · picnic · camp · view · food · elevation 610' trail · jeep trail · dirt · paved · rr grade · stream

To McCleary

8

To Olympia, Interstate 5

540'

N

B-Line

C a p i t o l

1

B-Line

B-1000 C-4000

C-4700

S t a t e

Rock Candy Mountain

20

C-5000

C-4000

To Get There:

From McCleary, travel 8 miles east on Hwy. 8 to the Rock Candy Mountain Entrance to Capitol State Forest on the right. Take this dirt road, the B-Line, one-quarter mile to a parking area. From Olympia and Interstate 5, travel north on Hwy. 101 then west on Hwy. 8 to the Rock Candy Mountain Entrance to Capitol State Forest on the left.

3

F o r e s t

40

3

Larch Mountain

30

2,280'

30

C-4000

0   ½   1
MILE

Capitol Peak

tain Loop is a long, strenuous ride which begins with a seven-mile climb on logging roads before traversing a series of technical, yet ridable, trails around Larch Mountain and then off the north side of Rock Candy Mountain.

Ride

From the parking area at the Rock Candy Trailhead, about one-quarter mile from Highway 8, begin riding west on the B-Line Road. The B-Line climbs gradually, traversing up along the northern base of Rock Candy Mountain. Stay on the main road, ignoring lesser roads on the left. Just before the **1.5-mile mark**, the road becomes steeper. Pass the North Rim Trail #1 on the left at **1.7 miles**.

After the **2-mile point**, the climb is more gradual. At **2.8 miles**, turn left onto road B-1000. At **3.3 miles**, take the upper, left fork on road C-4000. Stay on C-4000, passing lesser roads on the right at **5.3 miles** and on the left at **6.2 miles**. At **7.3 miles**, reach the trailhead at a 4-way intersection.

As you enter the intersection, veer to the right and look for the Mt. Molly–Porter Trail #3. Pass a trail that runs back to the left at **7.5 miles**, and continue up (climbing, traversing, then climbing) the sometimes technical single track as it winds along the north flank of Larch Mountain. When the trail forks at **10.8 miles**, take the left fork onto Trail #30 toward Capitol Peak.

Trail #30 climbs a short ways, then crosses a road at **11.2 miles**. The trail traverses the south flank of Larch Mountain until dropping to Road C-4000 at **12.7 miles**. Turn left on the road. Just around the bend, find Trail #30 on the southeast corner of the 3-way intersection of roads—go left on the trail, away from the trail to Capitol Peak. At **13.4 miles**, continue on Trail #30, passing two trails on the left.

After descending a series of steep switchbacks, reach a 4-way intersection at **13.8 miles**—turn left onto the Mt. Molly Loop Trail #40. After a pleasant traverse, the trail becomes quite wide, part of an old logging railroad grade. When the trail meets a road at **15.3 miles**, stay on the trail, right. At **15.6 miles**, select the right fork, which is Trail #20.

From this fork, take the next two left turns—at **15.8** and **15.9 miles**—staying on Trail #20. From here, the trail is quite technical in places, with some short but steep hills thrown in for good measure. Cross a road to the trail on the opposite

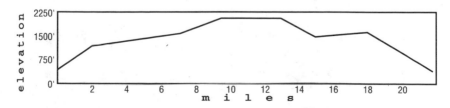

side at **17.3 miles** and then again at **18.1 miles**. Just past the second road crossing, take the right fork, away from Rock Candy Peak.

From here, the trail descends a series of raucous switchbacks. Cement pavers have been embedded into the trail at many of the hairpins to prevent erosion. At **19.2 miles**, meet a road. Turn left, and then immediately take the North Rim Trail off to the right. Veer to the left onto a wide trail at **19.6 miles**. Then at **20.2 miles**, reach B-Line Road to complete the loop. From here, turn right and ride down the road to the Rock Candy Trailhead, **21.9 miles**.

Trail riding with a companion

MORE RIDES

Whistler

Dozens of miles of trails zigzag across the mountains and valleys near Whistler. In addition to the rides included in this book (pages 40 and 42), I'd suggest riding the cross-country ski trails near Lost Lake. If you have plenty of route-finding patience, it's possible to ride from Whistler to Squamish almost entirely on soft-surface trails and roads on the Sea-to-Sky Trail. Then you can tell your friends the first 30 miles of your Pacific Coast tour was done on dirt. For more information, call SportStop in Whistler Village, ☎ 604-932-5495.

Anacortes

In addition to Cranberry Lake (page 51), plenty of other rides exist on Anacortes Community Forest Lands (ACFL), either near Cranberry Lake or in the Whistle Lake/Heart Lake area. Off the thoroughfares, trails in both areas are challenging and beautiful. For more information, call ☎ 360-293-1918.

Olympic National Forest

Hood Canal bounds much of the eastern edge of the Olympic National Forest (see rides page 54 and 56). To reveal even more mountain bike mysteries hidden within, stop by the Quilcene Ranger Station just south of Quilcene on Highway 101. Be aware, the maps they hand out may be inaccurate. For more information, call the Hood Canal Ranger District, ☎ 360-877-5254.

Kitsap Peninsula

Although the Kitsap Peninsula is slightly off the touring route, excellent riding can be found on Washington State Department of Natural Resources (DNR) land there. Tahuya State Forest and Green Mountain State Forest both have many miles of great single-track riding. For more information, check out *Kissing the Trail: Greater Seattle Mountain Bicycle Adventures* by John Zilly.

Capitol Forest

Capitol State Forest is another large Washington State DNR forest that allows mountain biking. In addtion to Larch Mountain, page 59, there are literally hundreds of miles of trails and dirt roads crisscrossing this area. The DNR prints a good map that is a must for any explorer, although it's hard to find.

THE OREGON
COAST

PRELUDE

I learned to fly with the sea gulls one morning near Beverly Beach, Oregon. I didn't fly with them in a new-age sense, I glided with them over the beach sands and their motion in the air carried me along. Although I was still on my bike, the secret of flying was mine.

I packed my pannier bags and, from the hiker/biker site at Beverly Beach Campground—south of Lincoln City and north of Newport—I rode south down the beach, right along the sand. Yaquina Head Lighthouse sat five miles in the distance. I watched the lighthouse and pedaled, freed, for once, from the job of scanning the road ahead for broken glass and pot holes. I didn't even have to ride in a straight line. None of this mattered on the beach. I felt as though I could ride this way all the way from Astoria to Brookings, the entire Oregon coast. But the lighthouse, warning ships of the rocky headland, reminded me that sandy beaches didn't line the entire coast. I was just south of Boiler Bay and Cape Foulweather, where waves crash into jagged sea stacks and explode—another Oregon coast classic.

I rode in the wet sand, just ahead of the fringe of foam at the edge of sea. I remembered being seven years old and running with a friend along the edge of the foam like that. One wave led to the next and our clothes were soon soaked. My friend's mother made us strip so she could dry our clothes in the sun before we hiked—three miles—back to the car later that afternoon. Despite the hot sun, we purged our embarrassment by donning heavy rain-coats and running willy-nilly across the sand.

This time, though, I did the prudent thing and kept my bicycle away from the salt water. Then I saw the sea gulls. Forty or fifty of them rested in the sand ahead. As I rode closer, they moved slightly, and then, so suddenly, they all went airborne at once, flying south to find another resting spot. They flew five to eight feet above the ground, gliding southward at the same speed I was going. I was among the flock, gliding with them, feeling the strength of their wings and the motion they made through the air. The smile I wore the rest of the day is legend.

Whistler

99

Canada
U.S.A.

British Columbia & Washington (p. 34)

101 Seattle

PACIFIC

Astoria

Washington
Oregon

Three Capes Tillamook

Portland

Oregon Dunes

North Bend

101

Elk River

Gold Beach

Oregon
California

101

California's Lost Coast (p. 90)

Fort Bragg

1

To the San Francisco Bay Area (p. 134)

San Francisco

Santa Cruz

OCEAN

Around Big Sur to Santa Barbara (p. 168)

1

Santa Barbara

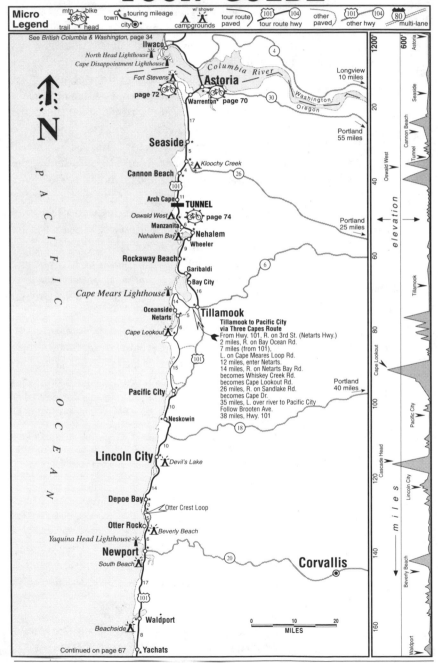

TOUR GUIDE

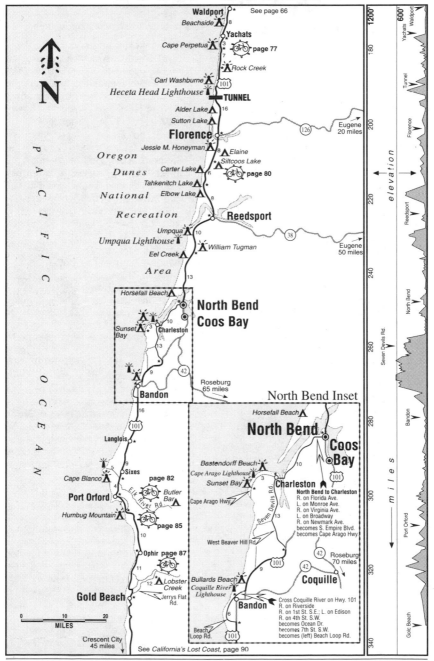

The following labels appear on the map:

N

Waldport ✶
See page 66
Beachside ⛺ 8
Yachats
Cape Perpetua ⛺ 🚲 page 77
7
✶ Rock Creek
Carl Washburne ⛺
Heceta Head Lighthouse ⛟
101
TUNNEL
Alder Lake ⛺ 16
Sutton Lake ⛺
126
Eugene 20 miles
Florence ✶

Oregon Dunes National Recreation Area

Jessie M. Honeyman ⛺ 8 ⛺ Elaine
✶ Siltcoos Lake
Carter Lake ⛺ 6 🚲 page 80
Tahkenitch Lake ⛺
Elbow Lake ⛺ 8
Reedsport
38
Umpqua ⛺ 10
Umpqua Lighthouse ⛟ ⛺ William Tugman
Eel Creek ⛺
Eugene 50 miles
13

Horsefall Beach ⛺
North Bend Coos Bay
⛺ 10
Sunset ⛺ 3 Charleston
Bay
13
⛺ 9 42
Bandon Roseburg 65 miles
16
101
Langlois ✶
9
✶ Sixes
Cape Blanco ⛟ 4 page 82
Butler Bar
Port Orford
Humbug Mountain ⛺
10
⛺ Ophir page 87
11 🚲 page 87
⛺ Lobster Creek
12 Jerrys Flat Rd.
Gold Beach ✶
Crescent City 45 miles

See *California's Lost Coast*, page 90

0   10   20
MILES

PACIFIC OCEAN

North Bend Inset

Horsefall Beach ⛺
North Bend
⛺ **Coos Bay**
Bastendorff Beach ⛺ 10
Cape Arago Lighthouse ⛟
Sunset Bay ⛺ 3 **Charleston** 101
Cape Arago Hwy.

North Bend to Charleston
R. on Florida Ave.
L. on Monroe Ave.
R. on Virginia Ave.
L. on Broadway
R. on Newmark Ave.
becomes S. Empire Blvd.
becomes Cape Arago Hwy.

West Beaver Hill Rd.
13
101
42
42 Roseburg 70 miles
Bullards Beach ⛺ 9
Coquille
Coquille River Lighthouse ⛟
Bandon
Cross Coquille River on Hwy. 101
R. on Riverside
R. on 1st St. S.E.; L. on Edison
R. on 4th St. S.W.
becomes Ocean Dr.
becomes 7th St. S.W.
becomes (left) Beach Loop Rd.
Beach 6
Loop Rd.
101

1200' 600'
Waldport
180 Yachats
Tunnel
200 Florence
elevation
220 Reedsport
North Bend
240
260 Seven Devils Rd.
Bandon
280
miles
Port Orford
300
320
340 Gold Beach

QUICK FACTS

miles (touring south from Astoria, Oregon)

0 **REPAIR:** Of the two bike shops in Astoria, **Bikes & Beyond** ☎ 503-325-2961 is the most helpful for both touring and mountain biking.

0 **RIDE:** If you're lucky, someone at Bikes & Beyond will explain the way to the **Weird Woods**, on the edge of town. (As the story goes, local riders call the woods "weird" because it's the only area that hasn't yet been logged.)

8 **CAMP & RIDE: Fort Stevens** ☎ 503-861-1671 is a large, bustling campground that you may want to skip in favor of a smaller camp down the coast. The mountain biking (page 72), the bicycle paths, and the showers are certainly a draw, but the bacon frying at every campsite, the flooded bathrooms, and the kids playing "chicken" on bicycles at 8 a.m. take away some of this campground's luster.

25 **SEE:** Though most of the trails in **Ecola State Park** are closed to bicycles, a couple of wide trails can be used by bicyclists to explore this rugged coastal park. Ask the park ranger.

26 **EAT:** The **Cannon Beach Bakery** bakes the most wonderful things, but they need to upgrade their coffee.

26 **REPAIR:** You haven't put in enough miles? Rent 3-wheeled recumbents for beach riding at **Mike's Bike Shop** ☎ 503-436-1266 in Cannon Beach.

32 **SLEEP:** The **Inn at Arch Cape** ☎ 503-436-0429 makes for a pleasant stay just before climbing over Cape Falcon.

39 **CAMP:** Tucked between two 500 ft. hills on Hwy. 101, **Oswald West** pro-

miles (touring south from Astoria, Oregon)

vides a great experience. The beach—Short Sands—is beautiful, and since the campground is a "walk-in only," the lack of RV traffic is welcome. Warning: protect your food from the raccoons, mice, blue jays, and squirrels.

45 **EAT & CUT:** Again for those who appreciate bizarre juxtapositions, enjoy a cinnamon roll and a haircut at the **Bakery/Barber shop in Wheeler**.

68 **SEE:** Tillamook's claim to fame: two cheese factories. Tours available.

68 **REPAIR: Drake's Bike Shop** is located at 2506 3rd in Tillamook.

68 **ROUTE:** From Tillamook south, the route down Hwy. 101 is shorter and less demanding than the hilly, though beautiful, **Three Capes Route** which includes Cape Mears Lighthouse.

88 **CAMP: Cape Lookout State Park** has a white sand beach and a hiker/biker camp, and it is located just north of the 700 ft. climb over Cape Lookout.

103 **EAT:** After crossing the strenuous Three Capes Route, the two bakeries in Pacific City will make even the most weary tourist smile. **Grateful Bread Bakery** ☎ 503-965-7337 sports a full menu including espresso; meanwhile, down the street, the **Colonial Bakery** sticks to the basics like foot-long maple bars and glazed donuts.

120 **REPAIR:** A garage door at a Lincoln City home will reveal a tiny bike shop if it looks like you might buy something. **Kats Bike Shop** ☎ 503-994-5242.

175 **EAT:** The sub-pronounceable town of Yachats is worth a short walking tour. No time? Stop by its two bakeries: **On The Rise** and **Morning Dew**.

178 **RIDE:** Rugged, foggy, and resistant to change, Cape Perpetua is one more incredible Oregon coast vista. From the visitor's center, check out the Cummins Creek ride, page 77.

183 **SLEEP:** Just south of Cape Perpetua, on a bluff that juts out into the Pacific, you'll find the **Sea Quest** ☎ 503-547-3782, an exquisite B&B. Elaine and George, the owners, like to say that the decor is garage sale, but it's much more cozy and sophisticated than that. And the views from the house are nothing short of awesome. The breakfasts are wonderful and filling; jacuzzis (most rooms) soothe tired muscles; the library and room journals allow for great escapes from life on the road. Bikes fit under the deck in the back.

186 **CAMP:** Although **Rock Creek** isn't the most beautiful campground on the coast, the two-story rock outhouse in the hiker/biker camp is unbelievable.

194 **SEE:** Finally, after all the bumper stickers, pass the **Sea Lion Caves**.

202 **EAT:** Florence has many restaurants.  For a tasty seafood dinner, try **ICM** at 1498 Bay St in "Old Town." For breakfast, try the often crowded **Blue Hen Cafe** at 1675 Hwy. 101 N. Although the "blue" and "hen" motifs have been exploited ad nauseam, this cafe provides bike racks, softball-sized muffins, and reasonable prices.

202 **SLEEP:** Also in the Old Town section of Florence, find **The Johnson House** ☎ 503-997-8000, a B&B with the feel of a European pension. Built in 1892,  Jayne and Ronald Fraese have restored the home to its original style. Jayne

cultivates a world-class herb garden for use in her excellent, if light, breakfasts. Bikes fit into the shed behind the house. Be sure to take off your cleats before walking around on the old wood floors.

210 **SEE: The Oregon Dunes National Recreation Area**, ☎ 503-271-3611, stretches from Florence to North Bend. As long as you don't get sand in your bottom bracket, it's a very cool place.

265 **SEE: The South Slough Estuary Interpretive Center** is located on Seven Devils Rd. about four miles south of Charleston. One of the most biologically diverse areas on the coast.

308 **SLEEP:** In the hamlet of Port Orford, an old fishing and timber community, you'll find **Home by the Sea**, a B&B run by Alan and Brenda Mitchell, ☎ 503-332-2855. Occasionally, pods of migrating whales venture into the cove between Port Orford Head and Humbug Mountain and can be seen from the Mitchell's property, which juts out into

the sea (thus the name). Laundry privileges and bike storage on the deck make it perfect for bicyclists. Alan has even driven to pick up weary bike tourists during bad storms. Find him on-line at 72672,1072@compuserve.com.

325 **SEE: Ophir**, a blip on the screen even while cycling, boasts a sausage-making company and raucous polka dances.

336* **SLEEP:** Bigger, less cozy, and pricier than some B&Bs, the **Tu-Tu-Tun Lodge** ☎ 503-247-6664 can nevertheless be recommended for the personal service, endless (and tasty) breakfasts, and hot tubs (some rooms) that overlook the beautiful and wild Rogue River.

337 **REPAIR:** Across the street from the Gold Beach Zoo (a pet store), find **Mike's Bicycles** at 180 3rd St.

*indicates site off tour route

CATHEDRAL TREE ✿✿✿

Checklist: 5 miles, Out & Back; dirt trail, paved road
Duration: 1–2 hours
Hill factor: lots of ups and downs
Skill level: advanced
Map: *City of Astoria*, Astoria Chamber of Commerce
Season: summer, fall
User density: high; cyclists, hikers
Explorability: high

Teaser

The route through Astoria to Cathedral Tree and the famous Astoria Column covers a hodgepodge of city streets, dirt roads, and technical dirt trails. Although the distance is short, the trails between Cathedral Tree, a 300-year-old Sitka Spruce, and the Column are not well maintained and quite technical in places, thus the three-wheel rating. Though the ride connects these two sights, the most exciting aspect to this ride is the amount of exploring possible. Lots of riding exists on the southeast side of Astoria, including the Weird Woods and many utility roads. But be sure to stop and enjoy the amazing views of the Columbia River from the Column.

Near Astoria Column, with the Astoria Bridge in the distance

CATHEDRAL TREE

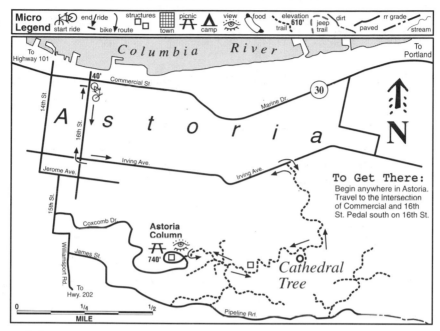

Ride

From the intersection of Commercial St. and 16th St., near the center of Astoria, take 16th St. south, up the steep hill. At **.4 mile**, turn left onto Irving Ave. and travel east. The road climbs, then descends to 28th St., at **1.2 miles**.

From the intersection of Irving St. and 28th St., turn right onto a dirt road. The road, which soon becomes more of a jeep trail, climbs into a dark forest. The road meets a boardwalk, **1.7 miles**; the boardwalk leads to Cathedral Tree, **1.8 miles**.

From the tree, the trail becomes quite narrow and rooted as it ascends west toward the Column. At **2.2 miles**, the way emerges from the forest and presents a myriad of possible routes. Ignore the lesser trails and roads to the right and left. Stay on the main trail which continues up. After a hectic climb up a steep, narrow trail—you may have to walk this stretch—reach the Astoria Column, **2.5 miles**. From here, retrace your pedal strokes to make the ride **5 miles**.

Alternatives

From the Column, you can also take Coxcomb Drive to 15th St. to return to Astoria. For more mountain biking, try any of the trails on the plateau below the Column (2.2 miles). To reach the Weird Woods, ride down Irving Ave. past 37th St. to the end of the pavement and take the second left off the dirt road. Prepare to become lost quickly.

FORT STEVENS ✺✺

Checklist: 6.1 miles, Loop; paved roads and paths, dirt trail alternative
Duration: 1–2 hours
Hill factor: mostly flat
Skill level: beginner
Map: *Fort Stevens Bicycle & Hiking Trails*, Oregon State Parks
Season: year round
User density: high; cyclists, pedestrians
Explorability: moderate

Teaser

Fort Stevens provides about 8.5 miles of paved bicycle paths. These trails lead to the Peter Iredale, the metal skeleton of a ship that wrecked in a storm in 1906, to the military museum that tells the history of the fort, and out to the picnic shelters at Coffenbury Lake. The trails are easy and generally flat.

Ride

From the ranger's booth at the entrance to the campground, find the paved bike path to the right. Riding west toward the beach, pass trails on the right and left at **.3 mile**. Immediately cross the road and continue on the bike path.

Hulk of the Peter Iredale beached at Fort Stevens

FORT STEVENS

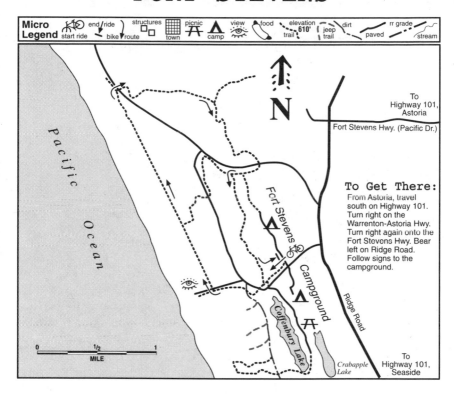

The path rejoins the road and parallels it for a time, but at **.9 mile**, turn right, crossing the road, and follow the bicycle path north as it parallels the beach. Pass a trail on the right at **1.5 miles**. At **2.8 miles**, turn right and immediately cross a road. Upon reaching a fork, **3.9 miles**, turn right (the left fork connects with the museum).

At **4.5 miles**, cross the road and then bear to the right. Take the second left at **4.8 miles**. Reach a T at **5.9 miles**, and turn left. Just down the trail, **6.2 miles**, complete the loop at the entrance booth.

Alternatives

From the entrance booth at the start of ride, pedal .3 mile along the paved bicycle path, cross the road, then turn left at the first dirt road, .4 mile. From here, there are three to four miles of trails that circle Coffenbury Lake. Be sure to avoid the hiking-only trails. Riding the beach at low tide between Fort Stevens and Gearhart presents another great alternative. This stretch of Oregon's coastline, about 12 miles one way, is also open to vehicle traffic.

NEAHKAHNIE MOUNTAIN ✿✿✿

Checklist: 8.6 miles, Out & Back; highway, dirt roads, dirt trail
Duration: 2–4 hours
Hill factor: very rigorous climb
Skill level: intermediate
Season: spring, summer, fall
User density: moderate; cyclists, hikers
Explorability: low

Teaser

Bicycles are not allowed on any of the trails in Oswald West State Park, thus the coastal trail, the trails on Neahkahnie Mountain, and even the paved paths to the campground are technically pedestrian only. Obviously we wish the use designations were different, but until they change, please respect them. This means walking your bike down to the campground and then locking your bike before hiking on the trails. There is, however, an old, gated dirt road that climbs up the south side of Neahkahnie Mountain. Some hiking is required to summit the mountain, but the struggle is well worth the breathtaking views. You wouldn't think climbing a 1600 ft. mountain would be so hard, or so visually rewarding.

Short Sands Beach, Oswald West State Park

NEAHKAHNIE MOUNTAIN

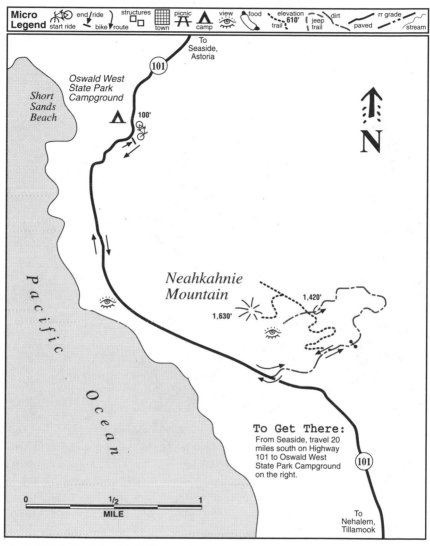

Micro Legend: end/ride • start ride • bike/route • structures • town • picnic • camp • view • food • elevation 610' • jeep trail • dirt • paved • rr grade • stream

To Seaside, Astoria

101

Oswald West State Park Campground

Short Sands Beach

△ 100'

Neahkahnie Mountain

1,420'

1,630'

To Get There:
From Seaside, travel 20 miles south on Highway 101 to Oswald West State Park Campground on the right.

101

To Nehalem, Tillamook

Pacific Ocean

0   1/2   1
MILE

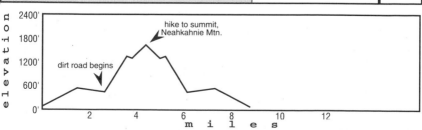

elevation: 2400' 1800' 1200' 600' 0'

hike to summit, Neahkahnie Mtn.

dirt road begins

miles: 2   4   6   8   10   12

View south from the top of Neahkahnie Mountain

Ride

Beginning at the parking area adjacent to the trail leading to Oswald West Campground, ride south on Highway 101. The highway, which may be congested during the summer, climbs steeply up the headland under Neahkahnie Mountain. Reach the summit, and some wonderful views, after climbing about 500 ft., **1.8 miles**. Roll off the top and coast downhill toward Manzanita, but at **2.3 miles**, turn left onto a dirt road.

Ride up the dirt road, passing a trailhead on the left at **2.7 miles**. The road continues its steep ascent; stay on the main road. At **3.1 miles**, pass through a gate and continue up. The route is quite steep from this point and walking may be the only solution. At **3.7 miles**, there's a short descent before another very steep climb.

Reach an intersection at **3.9 miles**. From this point, stash your bikes and walk up the trail about one-half mile to the top of the mountain and the spectacular views, **4.3 miles**. From the top, turn around and retrace your steps.

CUMMINS CREEK ✺✺✺✺

Checklist: 10.4 miles, Loop; paved road, dirt trail, jeep trail
Duration: 2–4 hours
Hill factor: long, relentless climb to begin
Skill level: advanced
Map: *Cummins Creek Wilderness*, USDA Forest Service
Season: summer, fall
User density: high; cyclists, hikers
Explorability: low

Teaser

Although most of the trails around Cape Perpetua are closed to bicycles, the Forest Service deserves credit for keeping the Cummins Creek Trail open because the trail is so close to the Cummins Creek Wilderness. The trail follows the edge of the Wilderness boundary as it winds through old growth stands toward the Pacific Ocean. Slightly over half this ride follows paved roads, but the exciting views of the ocean and the fun trail make up for it. In fact, it's a blessing that the first half of the route is paved, because it makes the 1500 ft. climb a little easier. The tough climb and the technical nature of the trail near the top mandate a four-wheel rating. Be courteous to other users and moderate your speed on the descent.

Near the bottom of Cummins Creek

Ride

From the Visitor's Center at Cape Perpetua, ride down the entrance road to Highway 101 and turn right. Northbound on Highway 101, take the first right turn onto Forest Service Road 55 at **.5 mile**. From here the long climb begins.

Pass the Cape Perpetua Campground, and then—**1.3 miles**—pass the road to Cape Perpetua Overlook (a sidetrip to the overlook adds 2 miles and 400 feet of climbing to the trip). Road #55 continues its steady, winding ascent. At **4.5 miles**, find a gravel parking area on the right. This is the Cooks Ridge Trailhead.

From the trailhead, pedal up the wide, grassy trail to a fork at **4.7 miles**. Take the upper, left fork—the Cummins Creek Trail. Crest the top of the ridge at **4.9 miles**, and then take the left, downhill fork at **5.1 miles**. For the next one-half mile, the trail descends precipitously and may have to be walked. At **5.3 miles**, take the right fork, following Cummins Creek Trail.

On a long bend to the right, the trail widens into a jeep trail and the grade becomes more gradual, **5.9 miles**. From here, the trail swings back and forth as it follows Cummins Creek along the edge of the Wilderness. At **8.4 miles**, the trail reaches a paved road. Follow the road down to Highway 101, **9 miles**. Turn right onto the highway and ride up to the entrance to the visitor's center on the right. Pedal up the hill to the visitor's center to complete the ride, **10.4 miles**.

CUMMINS CREEK

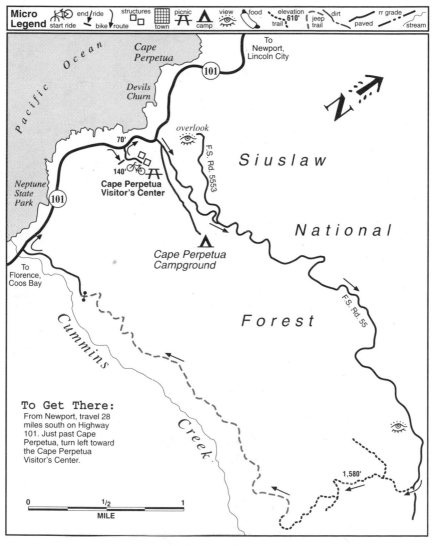

Micro Legend — end ride, start ride, bike route, structures, town, picnic, camp, view, food, elevation 610' trail, jeep trail, dirt, paved, rr grade, stream

Pacific Ocean

Cape Perpetua

Devils Churn

To Newport, Lincoln City

101

overlook

70'

140'
Cape Perpetua Visitor's Center

Neptune State Park

101

To Florence, Coos Bay

Cape Perpetua Campground

F.S. Rd. 5553

Siuslaw

National

Forest

F.S. Rd. 55

Cummins

Creek

1,580'

To Get There:
From Newport, travel 28 miles south on Highway 101. Just past Cape Perpetua, turn left toward the Cape Perpetua Visitor's Center.

0   1/2   1
MILE

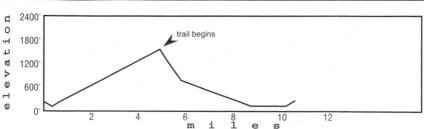

elevation — 2400', 1800', 1200', 600', 0' — trail begins — 2, 4, 6, 8, 10, 12 — miles

SILTCOOS LAKE ❁❁❁

Checklist: 4 miles, Out & Back; dirt trail
Duration: 1 hour
Hill factor: rolling, some short climbs
Skill level: intermediate
Season: spring, summer, fall
User density: very high; cyclists, hikers
Explorability: low

Teaser

Located south of Florence, Oregon, the lovely Siltcoos Lake sits a couple of miles inland from the ocean, just across the state's vast sand dunes. The single-track trail winds and rolls through dark forests down to a number of primitive campsites along the lake. This is a short ride, though the trail is, at times, technical, thus the three-wheel rating. For experienced cyclists touring down the coast, this trail would present little problem, even with panniers.

The Siltcoos Lake Trail starts from Highway 101

SILTCOOS LAKE

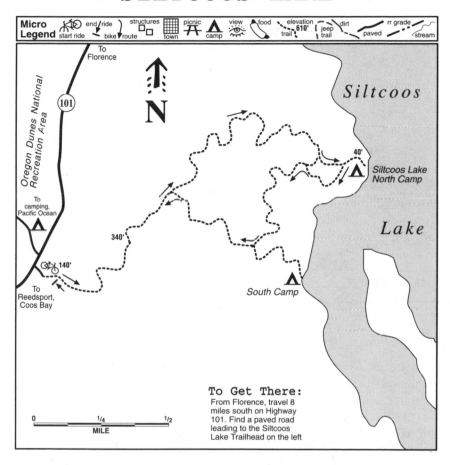

Micro Legend: start ride / end ride, bike route, structures / town, picnic, camp, view, food, elevation 610' / trail, jeep trail, dirt / paved, rr grade / stream

To Florence

101

Oregon Dunes National Recreation Area

Siltcoos

40'

Siltcoos Lake North Camp

To camping, Pacific Ocean

340'

Lake

140'

To Reedsport, Coos Bay

South Camp

0   ¼   ½
MILE

To Get There:
From Florence, travel 8 miles south on Highway 101. Find a paved road leading to the Siltcoos Lake Trailhead on the left

Ride

From the Siltcoos Lake parking area, eight miles south of Florence on the east side of Highway 101, take the widish dirt trail. The trail rises gradually away from the parking area, into a dark forest. After topping out just past **.5 mile**, the way drops to a fork at **.8 mile**. Take the upper trail on the left. The route rolls as the trail descends toward the lake. Just before the **2-mile mark**, stay on the main trail to the left. At **2 miles**, reach Siltcoos Lake and the primitive camp sites.

To return, either retrace your steps, or take the south route by taking the first left as you leave the lake. Returning via the south route, take a right at a fork in the trail, **2.5 miles** (a left goes to more primitive sites at the south camp). At **3.2 miles**, after climbing a hill, arrive at a fork. Turn left to return to the parking area. Climb to the top, and then finish the ride at **4 miles**.

ELK RIVER ✽✽

Checklist: 38 miles, Out & Back; paved road
Duration: 3–5 hours
Hill factor: gradual climb
Skill level: beginner
Map: *Siskiyou National Forest*, USDA Forest Service
Season: year round
User density: low; cyclists, vehicles
Explorability: high

Teaser

For those staying in Port Orford wishing for an easy, though long, ride that doesn't overstress the quadriceps, indulge in the Elk River Road. The road winds gently up the south side of the Elk River—one of the most potent rivers on the Pacific coast for naturally spawning salmon—toward several primitive campgrounds and hundreds of miles of logging roads beyond. Just across the river, the Grassy Knob Wilderness Area rises up from the north bank. Small in size but large in heart, the Grassy Knob Wilderness is a monument to the work of a few dedicated locals who prevented the Forest Service from punching a hole through the center of the roadless area before Wilderness designation came. Needless to say, the Elk River, a National Scenic River, makes for a lovely excursion.

Elk River near Grassy Knob Wilderness

ELK RIVER

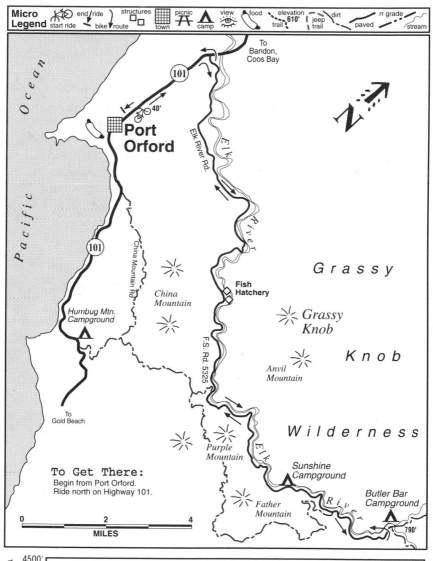

Micro Legend: end/ride · start ride · bike route · structures · town · picnic · camp · view · food · elevation 610' · jeep trail · dirt · paved · rr grade · stream

To Bandon, Coos Bay

101

Port Orford

40'

Elk River Rd.

Elk River

Ocean

Pacific

China Mountain Rd.

101

China Mountain

Fish Hatchery

G r a s s y

Grassy Knob

K n o b

Humbug Mtn. Campground

F.S. Rd. 5325

Anvil Mountain

To Gold Beach

W i l d e r n e s s

Purple Mountain

To Get There:
Begin from Port Orford.
Ride north on Highway 101.

Sunshine Campground

Father Mountain

Butler Bar Campground

790'

```
0        2        4
    MILES
```

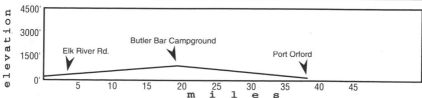

elevation: 4500' · 3000' · 1500' · 0'

Elk River Rd.

Butler Bar Campground

Port Orford

miles: 5 10 15 20 25 30 35 40 45

Ride

Beginning from Port Orford, ride north on Highway 101. At **3 miles**, turn right (east) onto Elk River Road. For the first few miles, the road keeps a distance from the river, affording views of Grassy Knob Wilderness. Some forests to the south of the river are still being logged, so watch for trucks. The road bears to the right and maintains a southeast tack for the rest of the way.

From the **6-mile point** the valley narrows and the road slips into sync with the bends of the river. At **10.7 miles**, pass a fish hatchery on the left. At **12.5 miles**, the road divides. Stay to the left along the river. (The right fork, which immediately becomes gravel, is the adventurous route back to Port Orford.)

At **16.5 miles**, cross a little bridge over an Elk River tributary. A deep hole in the river marks the spot. At **17.8 miles**, pass the Sunshine Campground tucked in a bend in the river on the left. At **19 miles**, reach the Butler Bar Campground. A picnic here or at Sunshine Campground is in order. Afterward, turn around and glide back to Port Orford to complete the ride, **38 miles**.

Alternative

If the gentle uphill grades and paved route of the Elk River Road seem too pedestrian for your tastes, try out the dirt roads to the south of Elk River. Some of these roads lead back to Humbug Mountain Campground and Port Orford, making an extremely long loop. The intense grades of these roads will exhaust any rider, so don't take them lightly. Buy a good map before heading out, and bring lots of water because the temperatures can be much warmer here (just a few miles inland) than on the coast.

OLD HIGHWAY 101 ✪

Checklist: 5.4 miles, Out & Back; old paved road, dirt road
Duration: 1 hour
Hill factor: gradual, steady climb
Skill level: beginner
Map: *Humbug Mountain State Park*, Oregon State Parks
Season: spring, summer, fall
User density: moderate; cyclists, hikers
Explorability: moderate

Teaser

This is one of the few sections of the Oregon Coast Trail (OCT) that bicycles are allowed on. Perhaps the reason is that this section of the OCT utilizes an abandoned section of the original Highway 101—two lanes and paved—but that would be cynical, wouldn't it? This old stretch of highway provides great views of the cove, sometimes called Whale Cove because of the gray whales that occasionally stop to rest on their migration. Also visible is Humbug Mountain, which rises conspicuously up from the Pacific to nearly 1,800 ft. The three-mile trail to the top of Humbug Mountain is open only to hikers because a bicyclist ran some hiker off the trail several years back. Just another story about one cyclist ruining it for the rest of us.

OLD HIGHWAY 101

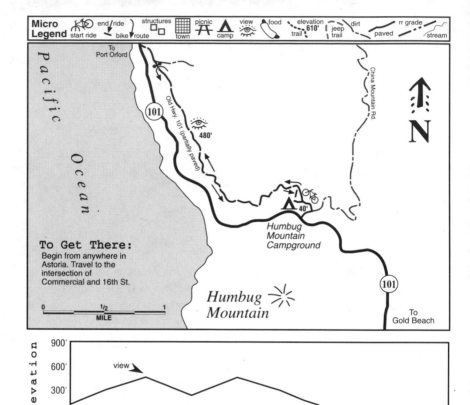

Micro Legend — end/ride, start ride, bike route, structures, town, picnic, camp, view, food, elevation 610', trail, jeep trail, dirt, rr grade, paved, stream

To Port Orford

Pacific Ocean

Old Hwy. 101 (partially paved)

China Mountain Rd.

480'

40'

Humbug Mountain Campground

To Get There:
Begin from anywhere in Astoria. Travel to the intersection of Commercial and 16th St.

Humbug Mountain

To Gold Beach

0   1/2   1
MILE

elevation: 900', 600', 300', 0'
miles: 1 2 3 4 5 6
view

Ride

From entrance booth at Humbug Mountain State Park, veer to the right, between the trailer dumping station and the ranger's compound. The old road climbs up next to the tiny Dry Run Creek. At **.2 mile**, the way becomes a gravel trail and then crosses a small bridge.

After the bridge, the route is paved again, although it's so old that grass grows through many cracks in the cement. During the ascent, watch for cove viewing sites. At **1.7 miles**, reach the top. From here, the road drops quickly to a gate at **2.5 miles.** Turn around here and retrace your steps to the campground to complete the ride, **5 miles**.

Just inland from Old Highway 101, hundreds of miles of logging road zigzag through the Siskiyou National Forest, making excellent, though often difficult, mountain bicycle routes.

LOWER ROGUE RIVER ✿✿✿✿

Checklist: 15.8 miles, Out & Back; paved road, dirt road, dirt trail
Duration: 3–5 hours
Hill factor: tough, short technical climbs
Skill level: advanced
Map: *Siskiyou National Forest*, USDA Forest Service
Season: spring, summer, fall
User density: moderate; cyclists, hikers, equestrians
Explorability: low

Teaser

Despite the fact the U.S. Forest Service recommends the Lower Rogue River Trail for bicycles, despite the fact that the *Oregon Gazetteer* recommends this trail for bicycles, despite the fact that other guide books recommend this trail for bicycles, the upper half of this trail is not a good mountain bike ride. Mountain biking is supposed to be enjoyable, but pushing your bike for hours up unridable trails isn't. The upper half of the Lower Rogue River Trail requires a lot more pushing than riding. But rather than omit this trail and let other sources mislead you, here is an amended, enjoyable version. The Rogue, a National Wild and Scenic River, is a lovely setting for a mountain bike ride. When glimpses of the river are available, soak them in. Watch out for poison oak and ticks.

LOWER ROGUE RIVER

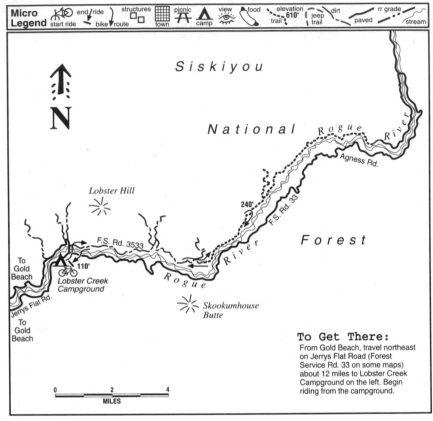

Micro Legend bike route start ride end ride structures town picnic camp view food elevation 610' trail jeep trail dirt paved rr grade stream

To Get There:

From Gold Beach, travel northeast on Jerrys Flat Road (Forest Service Rd. 33 on some maps) about 12 miles to Lobster Creek Campground on the left. Begin riding from the campground.

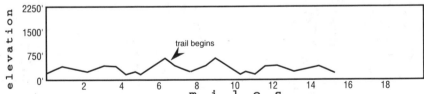

Ride

Begin at the intersection of Jerrys Flat Road and the entrance to Lobster Creek Campground. Pedal east on the Jerrys Flat Road. At **.1 mile**, following the signs to Lower Rogue River Trail, turn left and cross the Rogue River.

Immediately after the bridge, turn right, up a steep, gravel hill. This is North Bank Road. After a time, the hill levels out a bit. Pass a hiking-only trail on the left that leads to the world's largest Myrtle tree (it's a five-minute walk).

The road undulates, dropping and climbing, with the Rogue River down below on the right. Stay on the main road, ignoring lesser roads on the right and left. When the road divides at **3.8 miles**, take the right fork that heads downhill. Take another right fork, following the signs for the Lower Rogue River Trail.

The road is paved for a short stretch, then turns to gravel again as it climbs a hill, **4.5 miles**. At **5.3 miles**, the road forks—take the left fork, again following the signs for the Lower Rogue River Trail. After crossing Little Silver Creek and climbing a very steep hill, **6 miles**, the road forks at a parking area just past the top of the hill.

This parking area is the trailhead for the Lower Rogue River Trail. The trail descends into an old, mixed forest—fir, myrtle, madrone, oak. At **7 miles**, the trail crosses an old dirt road. Cross the road to the trail on the opposite side.

The trail narrows and rollercoasters along, with some steep sections; the river is visible below through the trees. At **7.9 miles**, cross the bridge at Slide Creek. I recommend turning around here and retracing your steps to Lobster Creek Campground, **15.8 miles**. If you have an adventurous spirit, the trail continues, although it never becomes more ridable.

The Rogue River

CALIFORNIA'S LOST COAST

PRELUDE

Whistler
99

British
Columbia &
Washington
(p. 34)

Seattle
101

Astoria

Washington
Oregon

Portland

PACIFIC

The
Oregon
Coast
(p. 64)

101

Gold Beach

Oregon
California

Crescent City

101

Eureka

The
Redwoods

The Lost
Coast

Jackson
State Forest

Fort Bragg

To The
San Francisco
Bay Area
(p. 134)

San
Francisco

Santa Cruz

OCEAN

Around
Big Sur to
Santa
Barbara
(p. 168)

Santa Barbara

It would be a lie if I said I didn't have a favorite restaurant on the Pacific coast. I found my bliss in Orick, way up on the northern California coast. A bustling timber community until recently, Orick is now known for the shops that sell chainsaw sculptures and redwood burls. At the south end of town, historical dates are displayed on the cross-section of a redwood tree that was healthy when Rome fell.

Using Elk Prairie Campground as a base camp, we had been mountain biking for several days in the redwoods, on the Ossagon Trail (page 102) and up Lost Man Creek (page 105). Later, touring south from the campground, named for the local herd of Roosevelt Elk, we were ready to discover the mysteries of the Lost Coast. In Orick, the conversation turned to food, specifically lunch. The choice was between the small grocery on the east side of Highway 101 and the Palm Cafe on the west side. The Palm seemed curiously misnamed; the slight drizzle closed the deal.

From the window seat we watched cars race past, lamenting the fact that the highway had become more crowded since Oregon. We wondered about touring the Lost Coast (page 118)—three intense days of touring (mountain biking?) dirt roads through the King Mountain Range, perhaps the most remote part of the Pacific coast.

I ordered the 18-Wheeler omelet—3 eggs, chili, and cheese—which came with 3 huge pancakes. Wade had the Bulldozer Burger. We split a big slice of banana cream pie, and then ordered another slice to be certain we completely overdid it. Normally, touring on a full stomach after lunch is not a problem; that afternoon it proved an epic struggle. Our pace was many miles per hour slower than usual.

Several days later, the radical mountain roads of the King Mountain Range tested our limits again. We averaged only 4 miles per hour. Calories were a top priority, and our small pannier bags weren't up to the task. We were short on food and hungry. After an unsatisfying dinner of camp-stovetop stuffing, the conversation drifted back to the Palm. "Could we have eaten any more that day?" "No way," Wade said. "But do you think they make Lost Coast deliveries?"

TOUR GUIDE

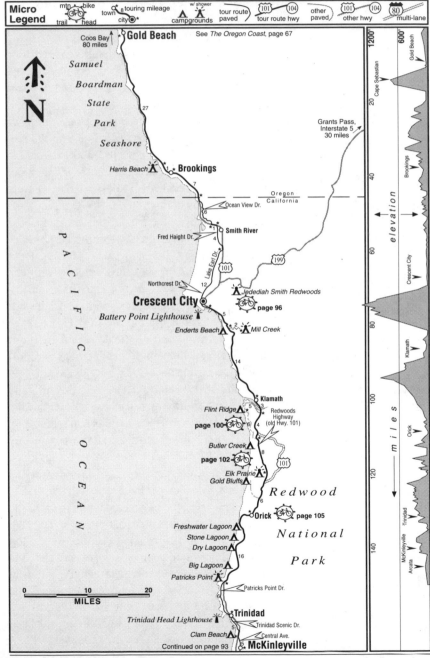

See *The Oregon Coast*, page 67

TOUR GUIDE

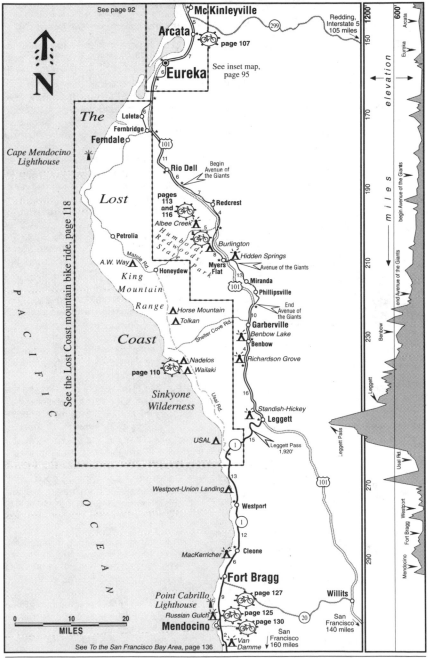

See page 92

McKinleyville

Arcata

299

Redding,
Interstate 5
105 miles

page 107

See inset map,
page 95

Eureka

The

Loleta

Fernbridge

Ferndale

101

Cape Mendocino
Lighthouse

Lost

Rio Dell

Begin
Avenue of
the Giants

pages
113
and
116

Redcrest

Albee Creek

Petrolia

Burlington

Hidden Springs

A.W. Way

Matole Rd.

Honeydew

Myers
Flat

Avenue of the Giants

King

Miranda

101

Mountain

Phillipsville

Range

Horse Mountain

Tolkan

End
Avenue of
the Giants

Coast

Shelter Cove Rd.

Garberville

Benbow Lake

Benbow

Nadelos

Richardson Grove

page 110

Wailaki

Sinkyone
Wilderness

Usal Rd.

Standish-Hickey

Leggett

USAL

1

15

Leggett Pass
1,920'

13

Westport-Union Landing

Westport

1

12

MacKerricher

Cleone

6

Point Cabrillo
Lighthouse

Fort Bragg

9

page 127

Willits

Russian Gulch

page 125

Mendocino

page 130

20

San
Francisco
140 miles

Van
Damme

San
Francisco
160 miles

N

PACIFIC

OCEAN

0   10   20
MILES

See the Lost Coast mountain bike ride, page 118

Humboldt Redwoods State Park

See *To the San Francisco Bay Area*, page 136

elevation

miles

1200'   600'

Arcata

Eureka

150

170

begin Avenue of the Giants

190

end Avenue of the Giants

210

Benbow

230

Leggett

Leggett Pass

Usal Rd.

270

Westport

Fort Bragg

290

Mendocino

QUICK FACTS

miles (touring south from Gold Beach, OR)

0   **EAT:** In addition to Mike's bike shop, the several supermarkets, and the many restaurants that grace Gold Beach, search out the **Gold Beach Bakery** located on Hwy. 101.

10   **SEE:** Perhaps the most classic stretch of Oregon's coast, Hwy. 101 treads the rocky cliff tops of **Samuel Boardman State Park Seashore**. Despite the constant fog and, while touring, the rigorous climbing between Gold Beach and Brookings, this is a beautiful stretch.

27   **CAMP:** Similar to most campgrounds on the Oregon coast and many on the California coast, **Harris Beach** has a nice hiker/biker site. One mile north of Brookings, this is the first campground on the touring route since Humbug Mountain, nearly 50 miles to the north.

28   **REPAIR: The Escape Hatch**, a bike shop and outdoor retailer, maintains stores in Brookings, ☎ 503-469-2914, and Crescent City, ☎ 707-464-2614.

35   **ROUTE:** Beginning at the California border, **Hwy. 101** becomes simulta-

miles (touring south from Gold Beach, OR)

neously narrower and more crowded. Take the non-highway route into Crescent City via Ocean View Dr., Fred Haight Dr., and Lake Earl Dr.

68   **INFORMATION:** Redwood National Park Headquarters located on the corner of 2nd and K Streets in Crescent City. Books and maps are available.

68   **MAP:** Trails Illustrated publishes an excellent map, *Redwoods National Park*, showing which trails and roads in the park are open to bicycles.

68   **READ:** Check out Bob Lorentzen's trail guide for California's north coast, *The Hiker's Hip Pocket Guide to the Humboldt Coast*. Despite the title, it also details mountain bike routes between Crescent City and the King Range National Conservation Area.

75   **CAMP: Mill Creek** is a lovely campground, tucked in the forests along Mill Creek. Unfortunately, the road to the campground descends over 600 ft. from Hwy. 101. This is fine at the end of the day, but with no warm up, the following morning's climb is hell.

90* **CAMP: Flint Ridge**, a walk-in campground slightly off the tour route, makes for a nice detour or tour-route alternative (page 100). Beware of the raccoons: They have acquired a taste for Power Bars and Dr. Bronner's soap.

102 **CAMP, RIDE, & SEE: Elk Prairie Campground** provides a good hiker/biker camp with a herd of Roosevelt Elk conveniently located in the field next to the hiker/biker site. Use the campground as a base camp for several mountain bike rides (pages 102, 105); if you time it properly, take in the annual Banana Slug Derby, in honor of those majestic creatures of the redwoods.

108 **EAT:** If the right cook happens to be working and the pies are fresh, there is no better place to be when hungry, wet, and tired than the **Palm Cafe** in Orick,

☎ 707-488-3381, on Hwy. 101. The Palm doubles as a motel, if you find yourself too stuffed to continue riding.

145 **REPAIR:** Find two good bike shops in Arcata: **Life Cycle** at 1593 G St., ☎ 707-822-7755, and **Adventure's Edge** at 650 10th St., ☎ 707-822-4673. Adventure's Edge also has a shop in Eureka at 408 F St., ☎ 707-445-3035.

145 **EAT:** There are a number of bakeries in Arcata; two provide the unique opportunity to ascertain what type of bakery person you are: **Don's Donut Bar**, 933 H St., is for the quantity people; **The Eureka Baking Company**, 846 G Street, is for the quality people.

153 **INSET MAP:** Eureka.

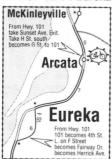

McKinleyville
From Hwy. 101
take Sunset Ave. Exit.
Take H St. south
becomes G St. to 101

Arcata

Eureka
From Hwy. 101
101 becomes 4th St.
L. on F Street
becomes Fairway Dr.
becomes Herrick Ave.

153 **REPAIR:** There are several bicycle shops in Eureka. If you are following the tour route, pass by **Henderson Center Bicycles** at 2811 F Street, ☎ 707-443-9861.

170* **SLEEP:** There may not be a more aptly named B&B on the coast than Ferndale's **Gingerbread Mansion Inn**, ☎ 707-786-4000. Even though the town sports many Victorian buildings, the Gingerbread Mansion is the most ornate and well-kept. The breakfasts are nice, but be sure to arrive before 4 p.m. when the innkeepers, Ken and Sandie Torbert, outdo themselves with afternoon tea (and treats), served in the mansion's parlors. Though off the tour route, Ferndale is a wonderful place to visit. It is also the place to stock up on

supplies to begin an assault of the Lost Coast. The Inn's historical scrapbook contains a photo of the Ferndale Bicycle Club, circa 1880, on a ride through

the country on fat-tired bikes. With the men dressed in suits and the women in long dresses, it's a hoot. Like all innkeepers, Torbert loathes grimy bike gear, cleats, and sleeping bags on the floor, so keep it clean. Reservations required.

187 **RIDE:** Despite the consistent wet fog that permeates the redwoods, don't miss the **Avenue of the Giants**. The Avenue, a peaceful, 30-mile stretch of road that parallels Hwy. 101, winds through Humboldt Redwoods State Park, passing grove after grove of the oldest living things on earth.

277 **EAT:** Whether emerging from the Lost Coast or touring over Leggett Pass from Hwy. 101, you'll appreciate the small grocery in **Westport**. It's small and spare, but it the first store in a while.

284 **EAT:** Hungry for breakfast? Try **Omelettes of Oz** on Hwy. 1 in Fort Bragg.

284 **REPAIR: Fort Bragg Cyclery**, ☎ 707-964-3509.

293 **RIDE: Mendocino Area Parks Assc.** (MAPA) prints a great whale-watching brochure. Gray whales summer in the Bering Sea, migrating south to Baja in the late fall and winter. If you are touring late in the year, or driving the coast, you may catch a glimpse of these behemoths as they travel south toward Baja.

293 **SLEEP:** Just a note for times when the weather is rotten or the campgrounds full: The California coast between Fort Bragg and Elk is littered with inns, B&Bs, and quaint motels. **The California Association of Bed & Breakfast Inns**, ☎ 800-284-4667.

*indicates site off tour route

BALD HILLS ✿✿✿✿

Checklist: 25.7 miles, Loop; dirt road, dirt trail, paved road
Duration: 4–6 hours
Hill factor: long, steep technical uphill; rocky, technical descent
Skill level: advanced
Map: *Redwood National Park*, Trails Illustrated
Season: spring, summer, fall
User density: medium; cyclists, walkers, equestrians, vehicles
Explorability: high

Teaser

The State of California and the National Park Service have created a patchwork of parks that preserve the coast's redwoods. This ride, over the Bald Hills, begins in Jedediah Smith Redwood State Park Campground, and progresses across Redwood National Park, before passing through Six Rivers National Forest. Just a few miles inland, the Bald Hills are much drier than the rain forests

Winding through a sparse pine forest near the top of Ball Hills

that line the Pacific coast. The sparse pine forests near the top are dry and can be hot. As always, watch for poison oak. The steep grade over the first third of the ride, the rough terrain on the drop into the south Fork of the Elk River, and the overall distance make this a four-wheel ride.

Ride

Begin this ride from the Jedediah Smith Campground. From the intersection of Highway 199 and the campground entrance, pedal west on Highway 199, which gradually climbs the Smith River Valley. After **2.3 miles** on the highway, reach a stoplight and turn right onto South Fork Road. The road immediately crosses the Smith River, curves for a time, then crosses the South Fork of the Smith River at **2.8 miles**.

The road divides just after the bridge. Take the right, following signs toward Little Bald Hills Trailhead. Pedal through an unusual covered bridge at **3.4 miles** as the road parallels the Smith River, heading west now, down river. At **4 miles**, enter Jedediah Smith Redwood State Park; the road turns from paved to dirt. When the road forks at **4.4 miles**, take the lesser road up to the left, the Little Bald Hills Trail. The trail, an old road, starts up steeply away from the river. After passing through a gate, the trail begins in earnest, narrower and rougher.

BALD HILLS

To Hwy. 101, Oregon

To Grants Pass, OR, Interstate 5

199

197

199
To Crescent City

140'
Jedediah Smith Campground

Jedediah Smith Redwoods State Park

South Fork Road

River

South Fork

Smith

Craigs Creek Mountain

Little Bald Hills Campground

Redwood National Park

Bald 1,990' Hills

Smith

River

Rock Creek

To Get There:

From Crescent City, take Highway 101 north. Turn east onto Highway 199. Proceed to Jedediah Smith Campground on the right. Begin the ride from the campground.

0   2   4
MILES

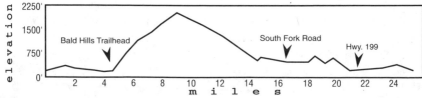

elevation: 2250' 1500' 750' 0'

Bald Hills Trailhead

South Fork Road

Hwy. 199

miles: 2 4 6 8 10 12 14 16 18 20 22 24

The trail, a wide single track, sets a steady climb. After climbing over 1200 ft., the trail enters a dry, sparse pine and hemlock forest, **6.9 miles**. Leveling occasionally, the trail continues its steep climb. Then at **7.8 miles**, the trail divides. The left fork leads to Little Bald Hills Campground, a primitive sight. Some bicyclists turn around here to enjoy the smooth single track they've just climbed up. (This makes the ride an Out & Back.)

To continue the loop, take the right fork which climbs gradually up the ridge. From the ridge, pass views west to the Pacific Ocean and east into the South Fork of the Smith River Valley. Just past the **9-mile mark**, after nearly 2,000 ft. of climbing, crest the top of the ridge. **Whoa**, at **9.6 miles**, the trail becomes difficult to follow as it passes through a meadow. By **9.9 miles**, the rocky trail has begun the steady descent into the South Fork of the Smith River Valley.

After a steep, rough, jeep-trail descent, it is necessary to ford Rock Creek, **14.5 miles**. From the creek crossing, climb the dirt road up the opposite bank to a T. Turn left and pedal down the dirt road. Reach the South Fork Road, **16.5 miles**, and turn left. The narrow, paved South Fork Road parallels the river.

At **22.9 miles**, the road divides—take the right fork (left leads back to the Little Bald Hills Trailhead). At **23.3 miles**, just after crossing a bridge over the Smith River, turn left onto Highway 199. From here, pedal west on the highway back to Jedediah Smith Redwoods Campground to complete the loop, **25.7 miles**.

South Fork Road

FLINT RIDGE ✪✪

Checklist: 10.6 miles, One Way; paved road, gravel road
Duration: 1–2 hours
Hill factor: several steep hills
Skill level: beginner
Map: *Redwood National Park Map & Guide*, National Park Service
Season: spring, summer, fall
User density: moderate; cyclists, vehicles
Explorability: low

Teaser

The road around Flint Ridge works as an easy mountain bike ride, but it also functions well as an alternative touring route to Highway 101. After passing the mouth of the Klamath River, the ride turns south and climbs the rocky headlands that rise out of the Pacific Ocean. If the fog burns off, several turnouts along the way afford views of the ocean crashing on the rocks below. The route is moderate in length and entirely on roads, but a few steep climbs make it a two-wheel ride.

Ride

Traveling south on Highway 101, take a hard right turn at the first exit immediately after crossing the Klamath River. The road, narrow, paved, and moderately trafficked, follows the river to its mouth. At a T, **.4 mile**, turn left. From here, stay on Coastal Drive (also known as B8 and Klamath Beach Road). At **1.9 miles**, continue straight through an intersection.

The road reaches a beach at the mouth of the Klamath River at **3.9 miles**. At this point, the road turns sharply to the left and heads up a very steep hill. Bicycle tourists will have to push here; mountain bikers may have to push as well. The road becomes gravel at **4.2 miles**. Find the trail to

FLINT RIDGE

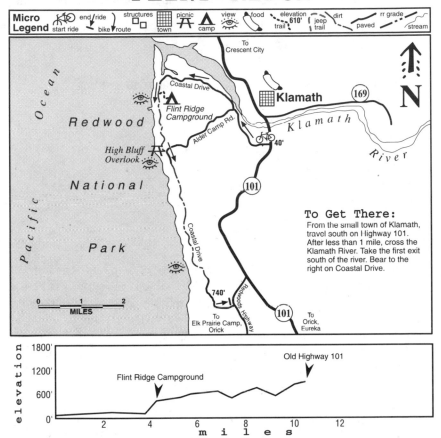

the Flint Ridge Campground on the left just as the road tops out near a gravel parking area. (The campground is about one-quarter mile from the road.)

From the parking area, which affords views of the rugged coastline, continue south. After dropping and then ascending again, the road becomes paved for a short time. The road, switching between gravel and paved, rollercoasters along the headland. Birds flit through the trees; banana slugs try to cross the road. Fog. Reach the High Bluff Overlook at **6 miles**.

Just past the overlook, the road reaches a T—turn right, following the signs for Highway 101, south. The road continues to oscillate between pavement and dirt. Pass another intense overlook, **8.9 miles**. The road slowly bends to the east and winds through a grove of giant redwoods. At **10.1 miles**, pass out of Redwood National Park and into Elk Prairie Redwood State Park. Reach Highway 101 at **10.6 miles** to complete the ride. Turn right to get to Elk Prairie Campground, 7.5 miles farther; turn left to return to the Klamath River to make a loop, 4 miles back.

OSSAGON TRAIL ✤✤✤

Checklist: 19.1 miles, Loop; paved road, dirt road, dirt trail
Duration: 2–3 hours
Hill factor: one long, sustained, grueling hill
Skill level: intermediate
Map: *Redwood National Park*, Trails Illustrated
Season: summer, fall
User density: high; cyclists, walkers
Explorability: low

Teaser

This ride allows bicyclists to sample a potpourri of riding surfaces and trail types, from paved highway to narrow, dirt trail. The loop begins from Elk Prairie Campground, drops down to the beach on a series of wide, dirt trails and a dirt road, and then winds along grassy bluffs before actually reaching the Ossagon Trail. The trail itself is generally wide, though quite steep (most riders will walk parts of it). But walking the Ossagon Trail isn't all bad since it passes through some incredible stands of old-growth redwood. Despite the length of the ride, it goes rather quickly as most of the route is on a dirt or paved road.

OSSAGON TRAIL

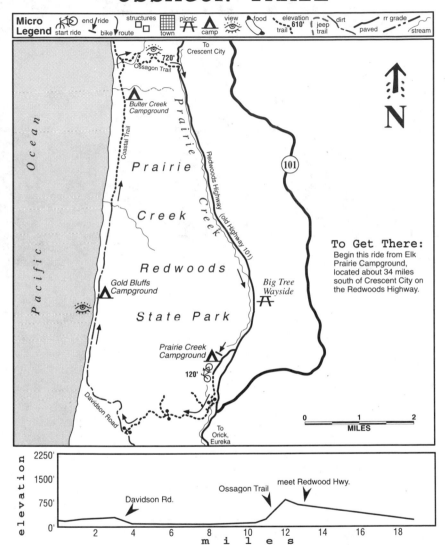

Micro Legend: start ride, end/ride, bike/route, structures, town, picnic, camp, view, food, elevation 610', trail, jeep trail, dirt, paved, rr grade, stream

To Crescent City

Ossagon Trail

Butler Creek Campground

Coastal Trail

Prairie Creek

Redwoods Highway (old Highway 101)

101

To Get There:
Begin this ride from Elk Prairie Campground, located about 34 miles south of Crescent City on the Redwoods Highway.

Gold Bluffs Campground

Big Tree Wayside

State Park

Prairie Creek Campground

120'

Davidson Road

To Orick, Eureka

0   1   2
MILES

N

Ocean

Pacific

elevation: 2250', 1500', 750', 0'

Davidson Rd.

Ossagon Trail

meet Redwood Hwy.

miles: 2, 4, 6, 8, 10, 12, 14, 16, 18

Ride

Beginning from the hiker/biker camp at Elk Prairie Campground, pedal south on the campground road, away from the entrance. Find the Jogging Trail, an old paved double track. Stay on the main trail. The trail turns to dirt, **.7 mile**, just before reaching a gate and a T. Turn right, following the little jogger signs.

Pass through another gate, and then at a fork, **.9 mile**, turn left, following the bicycle signs. This jeep trail rollercoasters through the woods, occasionally on

Crossing Ossagon Creek near Gold Bluffs Beach

pavement from the old road. When the trail forks again, take a second left. The trail narrows at times, and the thick, lush canopy makes it feel like a tunnel.

At **3 miles**, pass through a gate and reach Davidson Road. Turn right on the road and climb for a short time before dropping sharply to the Pacific Ocean, **4.7 miles**. At some point as Davidson Road heads north, it becomes Gold Bluffs Road, which is rougher and narrower. Pass the Gold Bluffs Campground at **6.6 miles**.

A herd of Roosevelt Elk frequent the grassy bluffs just in from the ocean. At **8.1 miles**, the road crosses a creek and ends at a parking lot. Immediately cross a second creek to the narrow trail on the opposite side. When the trail divides, stay on the Coastal Trail to the left, following the signs to the Ossagon Trail. Cross another stream and then watch for the waterfall up to the right.

Other than one bog that will slow travel, the hard-packed single track winds through the grasses of the upper beach. Pass the primitive Butler Creek Camp at **10.5 miles**. Stay on the Coastal Trail. At **10.9 miles**, after crossing another creek, the Ossagon Trail forks to the right into the forest and begins a double black-diamond climb. Many riders will walk much of the next mile.

Banana slugs inch out of the fern, alder, and redwood forest. After a short, tough climb and a short walk down a set of stairs, the real grind begins. But as you go into severe oxygen debt, don't miss the beautiful redwood forest on this climb to Highway 101. The trail levels out at **12.2 miles** and then drops to the highway, **12.6 miles**. Turn right onto Highway 101 and pedal downhill, back to Elk Prairie Campground to complete the loop at **19.1 miles**.

LOST MAN CREEK ✸✸✸✸

Checklist: 21 miles, Out & Back; dirt road
Duration: 3–4 hours
Hill factor: long sustained climb for entire first half
Skill level: beginner
Map: *Redwood National Park*, Trails Illustrated
Season: year round
User density: moderate; cyclists, walkers, equestrians
Explorability: low

Teaser

Mountain bicycles are not allowed on trails in U.S. National Parks. But rangers in Redwood National Park and California's redwood state parks have done a good job of keeping some non-motorized routes open to bicycles. Many of the rides in this section travel through redwood forests, many of them old-growth stands. Lost Man Creek is just such a ride. After edging away from the creek, the road acquires Holter Ridge and continues climbing, almost without pause, to the turn-around point. Although the route traverses a non-technical, old dirt road the entire way, the 2000 ft. elevation gain makes this a difficult ride.

Redwood National Park

LOST MAN CREEK

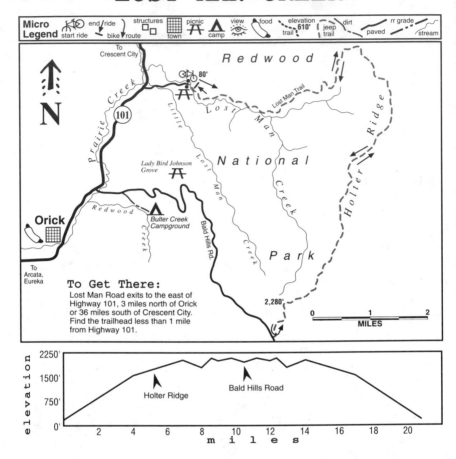

Ride

From the parking area at the end of the pavement, begin riding up the road beyond the gate. For the first mile, the road parallels Lost Man Creek. Just after the **1-mile mark**, the road edges away from the creek and begins climbing in earnest.

After 1300 ft. of climbing, at **4 miles**, the road bends to the right and heads south—still ascending—along Holter Ridge. From here, the road parallels the park boundary as it climbs the ridge. All the way up, stay on the main road. At **10 miles**, reach the top of the ride. Drop to Bald Hills Road, which is paved, at **10.5 miles**. From here, turn around and retrace your pedal strokes, making the ride **21 miles**. (A loop can be made by turning right on Bald Hills Road, gliding down to Highway 101, turning right and then turning right again at Lost Man Road.)

COMMUNITY FOREST ⊛⊛

Checklist: 4.2 miles, Loop; dirt trail, dirt road
Duration: 1–2 hours
Hill factor: rolling hills, some steep sections
Skill level: intermediate
Map: *Arcata Community Forest*, Arcata Environmental Services
Season: spring, summer, fall
User density: high; cyclists, runners, walkers, equestrians, some vehicles
Explorability: high

Teaser

Arcata Community Forest is a wonderful place on a number of counts: The forest is adjacent to town, it has seven miles of roads and trails open to mountain bicycles, and it is a lovely forest, despite the powerlines that run through it. **Whoa**, this is a great place, but it has an extremely high amount of use so be careful and courteous. On some of the downhills, trenches have been dug to divert water but also to slow bicyclists down. Most of the riding is not too technical, but there are a few stiff climbs and possibly some walking.

A wide trail, Arcata Community Forest

Pedaling up a steep hill in Arcata's Community Forest

Ride

Beginning from the trailhead at the end of California St., pedal out the narrow Trail #5. The trail, which climbs into the forest, hairpins to the right soon after it begins. At **.4 mile**, the trail reaches a dirt road at a T. Turn left onto Trail #8 and continue climbing up the road.

The road divides quickly; take the left fork onto Trail #11, which levels somewhat. When the road divides again, **.8 mile**, turn right, staying on Trail #11. From here, the road traverses for a time before descending to Jane's Creek. Ignore the pedestrian-only trail on the right. After crossing the creek, the road climbs, bends to the right and passes under a set of powerlines, and then continues to climb.

Stay on the main road, ignoring a road on the left and then on the right. Just prior to the **2-mile mark**, hit the top of the hill. At **2 miles**, the way forks—take the right fork onto Trail #7.

Trail #7, a narrow, more technical route, drops swiftly back into Jane's Creek drainage. After crossing the creek, the trail climbs easily up to a T, **2.3 miles**. Turn right here onto the dirt road, Trail #12. This road makes a high traverse, passes

COMMUNITY FOREST

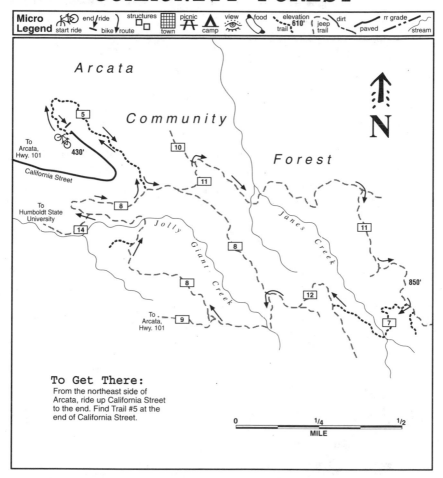

To Get There:
From the northeast side of Arcata, ride up California Street to the end. Find Trail #5 at the end of California Street.

the trail up to the right, then drops to reach Trail #8, the Community Forest Loop Road at **2.7 miles**.

Turn left onto Trail #8. From here, the road descends to Jolly Giant Creek. After crossing the creek, the road climbs slightly, then passes under a set of powerlines just before a complicated 3-way intersection. Stay on Trail #8 by keeping to the right after the powerlines. From this point, the road crests a hill, then drops to cross Jolly Giant Creek a second time. Meanwhile, stay on the main road, Trail #8.

When the road forks, stay to the right on Trail #8. Soon afterward, the road hairpins to the right and climbs to the intersection with Trail #5, **3.8 miles**. From here, turn left onto Trail #5 and pedal down the narrow trail until it deadends at California St. This completes the loop, **4.2 miles**.

CHEMISE MOUNTAIN ✿✿✿

Checklist: 4.6 miles, Loop; dirt trail, dirt road
Duration: 1–2 hours
Hill factor: a few tough, technical grades, some walking
Skill level: advanced
Map: *Trails of the Lost Coast*, California Coastal Foundation
Season: summer, fall
User density: moderate; cyclists, hikers, equestrians
Explorability: low

Teaser

Though short, the ride out to Hidden Valley and up the slopes of Chemise Mountain is difficult: steep and sometimes quite technical. Thus the three-wheel rating in spite of the distance. But Hidden Valley is beautiful, and a herd of Roosevelt Elk frequent it. Indeed, views of the Pacific from the flanks of Chemise Mountain are inspiring.

Hidden Valley at dusk

CHEMISE MOUNTAIN

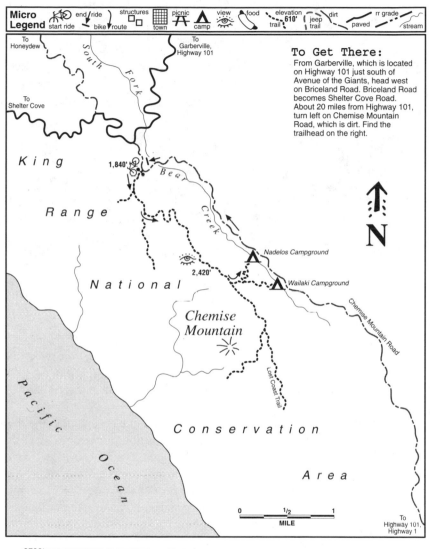

Micro Legend: end ride, start ride, bike route, structures, town, picnic, camp, view, food, elevation 610' trail, jeep trail, dirt, paved, rr grade, stream

To Honeydew

To Garberville, Highway 101

To Shelter Cove

To Get There:
From Garberville, which is located on Highway 101 just south of Avenue of the Giants, head west on Briceland Road. Briceland Road becomes Shelter Cove Road. About 20 miles from Highway 101, turn left on Chemise Mountain Road, which is dirt. Find the trailhead on the right.

King Range National Conservation Area

South Fork

Bear Creek

1,840'

N

2,420'

Nadelos Campground

Wailaki Campground

Chemise Mountain

Chemise Mountain Road

Lost Coast Trail

Pacific Ocean

0   1/2   1
MILE

To Highway 101, Highway 1

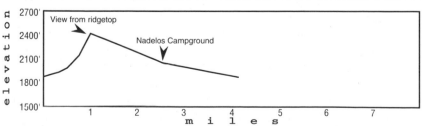

elevation: 2700', 2400', 2100', 1800', 1500'

View from ridgetop

Nadelos Campground

miles: 1 2 3 4 5 6 7

Private site at Nadelos Campground

Ride

From the small parking area at the Hidden Valley Trailhead, from which the Chemise Mountain Trail and the Lost Coast Trail also begin, ride past the gate, following the signs for Chemise Mountain. Just after the gate, the road narrows to single track.

At **.3 mile**, the trail reaches a grassy meadow, a grazing spot for a herd of Roosevelt Elk in the area. The trail forks just after meeting the meadow—take the lesser trail up to the left. When the trail divides again, **.5 mile**, take the left fork, following the signs for Chemise Mountain. The trail enters a dense thicket and immediately begins switchbacking up the north flank of Chemise Mountain. Sections of these switchbacks are quite steep and will require some walking.

Gain the ridge at **1.5 miles**; from here, the trail is less severe. As the trail rides the top of the ridge, pass several great views of the Pacific Ocean. At **2.5 miles**, after a short descent, arrive at a fork. The right fork leads up to the top of Chemise Mountain. Instead, turn left and switchback down to Nadelos and Wailaki Campgrounds. The trail divides on the way down the hill—turn left toward Nadelos Campground.

After more steady downhill, reach the campground at **3.1 miles**. Ride through the camp to the main dirt road. Turn left at the road and ride, slightly downhill, back to the Hidden Valley Trailhead to complete the ride, **4.6 miles**.

WHISKEY FLAT ✪✪✪

Checklist: 14.6 miles, Loop; dirt road, paved road
Duration: 2–4 hours
Hill factor: a few tough grades
Skill level: intermediate
Map: *Humboldt Redwoods State Park*, California Dept. of Parks
Season: spring, summer, fall
User density: moderate; cyclists, hikers, equestrians, vehicles
Explorability: high

Teaser

Beginning near Albee Creek Campground, this ride winds around the west side of Grasshopper Peak on a series of old dirt roads, through epic redwood groves, to Whiskey Flat Camp, named for the still that cranked out whiskey during Prohibition. Beyond the camp, the roads plunges down into Bull Creek Valley and easily descends back to Albee Creek. The steep grades before and after Whiskey Flat and the rough and tumble descent down—ironically—Preacher Gulch make this a difficult ride, despite riding on roads the entire way.

Views into the fog from Preacher Gulch Road

Ride

From the intersection of Mattole Road and Grasshopper Road, pedal up Grasshopper Road. **Whoa**, Grasshopper Road, a gravel-and-dirt fire road, is easy to miss; it's located to the south just west of the bridge across Bull Creek. Ride up Grasshopper Road through several gates. At **.6 mile**, pass an unmarked road on the right, continuing up the main road.

At **.8 mile**, the road divides: take the right fork, following the signs toward the Squaw Creek Ridge Road. The road alternately climbs and traverses. Just past the **1-mile mark**, it rises quickly past a grove of enormous redwoods. Pass an environmental camp off on the right at **2.7 miles**. The pleasant dirt and pine-needle road rises gently past more redwoods, which frustrate views of the Bull Creek Valley.

Reach Whisky Flat Environmental Camp, **4.7 miles**. From here, the way becomes quite steep. After a tough grind, arrive at an intersection at the top of the hill, **6.3 miles**. Turn left toward Bull Creek Camp and immediately begin descending. At **6.7 miles**, reach a fork. Turn right onto Preacher Gulch Road, continuing toward Bull Creek Road. Rough and less maintained, Preacher Gulch Road drops precipitously to its confluence with Bull Creek Road, **8.6 miles**.

At Bull Creek Road, turn right and ride down the wide, dirt road. Pass Bull Creek Trail Camp at **8.8 miles**. From here, the road parallels Bull Creek as it gradually descends to the Mattole Road, at **12.3 miles**. Turn right on this paved road and ride back to Grasshopper Road, **14.6 miles**, to complete the loop.

WHISKEY FLAT

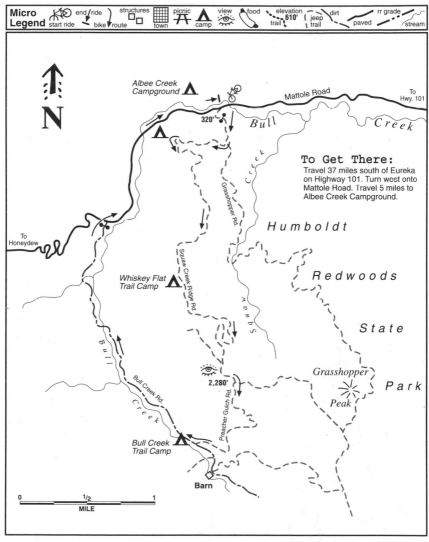

Micro Legend: end ride / start ride · bike route · structures / town · picnic · camp · view · food · elevation 610' trail · jeep trail · dirt · paved · rr grade · stream

Albee Creek Campground

320'

Mattole Road

To Hwy. 101

Bull Creek

To Get There:
Travel 37 miles south of Eureka on Highway 101. Turn west onto Mattole Road. Travel 5 miles to Albee Creek Campground.

To Honeydew

Grasshopper Rd.

Humboldt

Redwoods

State

Squaw Creek Ridge Rd.

Whiskey Flat Trail Camp

Squaw Creek

2,280'

Grasshopper Peak

Park

Bull Creek Rd.

Bull Creek

Preacher Gulch Rd.

Bull Creek Trail Camp

Barn

0   1/2   1
MILE

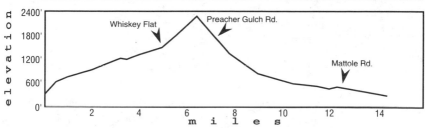

Elevation profile: elevation (0' to 2400') vs. miles (2 to 14)

Whiskey Flat · Preacher Gulch Rd. · Mattole Rd.

BULL CREEK ✪

Checklist: 8 miles, Out & Back; dirt road
Duration: 1–2 hours
Hill factor: gentle grades
Skill level: beginner
Map: *Humboldt Redwoods State Park*, California Dept. of Parks
Season: spring, summer, fall
User density: moderate; cyclists, hikers, equestrians
Explorability: moderate

Teaser

For an easy ride in the Humboldt Redwoods, try the route up Bull Creek. This ride provides access to some much more difficult riding (hill climbing) up to Perimeter Road and Grasshopper Peak. But for beginning mountain bikers, this is a pleasant ride up the Bull Creek Valley. The wide, well-maintained road and gentle grades make it a one-wheel ride. The open, grassy route allows for views of the surrounding mountains, though the lack of shade can make it a hot ride during the summer.

Ride

From Mattole Road, ride up Bull Creek Road. For most of the way, the road rises gently toward Bull Creek Trail Camp, although a couple of stretches prove steeper.

The road, which is wide and nicely compacted dirt, parallels Bull Creek as it winds up the open grassy valley. Cross the creek at **1.7 miles**. At **3.4 miles**, pass the Bull Creek

BULL CREEK

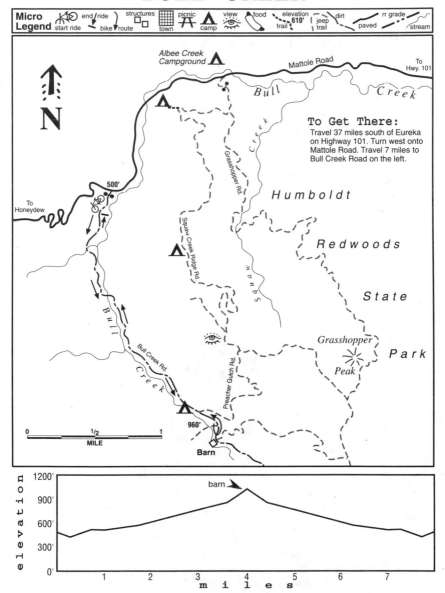

start ride — end/ride — bike route — structures — town — picnic — camp — view — food — elevation 610' — trail — jeep trail — dirt — paved — rr grade — stream

Albee Creek Campground

Mattole Road

To Hwy. 101

Bull Creek

To Get There:
Travel 37 miles south of Eureka on Highway 101. Turn west onto Mattole Road. Travel 7 miles to Bull Creek Road on the left.

Humboldt

Redwoods

State

Park

Grasshopper Peak

500'

To Honeydew

Bull Creek

Grasshopper Rd.

Squaw Creek Ridge Rd.

Squaw Creek

Bull Creek Rd.

Preacher Gulch Rd.

960'

Barn

0   1/2   1
MILE

Trail Camp. Pass Preacher Gulch Road on the left at **3.6 miles**. Then pass Kemp Road on the right a short time later.

Stay on the main road. Reach picturesque Lower Gould Barn at **4 miles**. Picnic here along the creek and then retrace your steps to Mattole Road to finish the ride, **8 miles**.

LOST COAST ✹✹✹✹✹

Checklist: 107 miles, One Way; dirt roads, paved roads
Duration: 3–5 days
Hill factor: many long, radically steep grades
Skill level: advanced
Map: *Trails of the Lost Coast*, California Coastal Foundation
Season: summer, fall
User density: low; occasional vehicle
Explorability: high

Teaser

You will hear lots of interesting comments about bicycling the Northern California's Lost Coast, from Loleta (south of Eureka) to Highway 1 (north of Fort Bragg). Some say it's impossible because the hills are too steep; others that

it's a "war zone" due to marijuana growing in the area; still others say there are no places to buy food or supplies. And there's a ring of truth to it all. This is the only multi-day mountain bike ride detailed in *Wild Pigs*, and on a number of levels, it's the most difficult, a true epic.

On our first day on the Lost Coast ride, we discussed the difficulty of the hills. Wade said: "You won't find this section a problem if you've completed the Tour de France several times." The ride got quite a bit more difficult after we left the pavement, tossing out numerous hurdles: radically steep grades over an endless series of hills;

An understated warning on the Usal Road

extra weight due to pannier bags loaded with food and spare parts; the intrinsic danger of remote places. Of course it's this remoteness and wildness that give this ride its beauty, intrigue, and challenge.

The Lost Coast ride works as an alternate to touring inland, on Highway 101 and the Avenue of the Giants. Since cars can drive the route, this can also be a vehicle-supported ride. (Of course all the same warnings go for your vehicle, too.) **Whoa** on two points: First, if you feel comfortable with 80-to 100-mile days on the road, figure on 30 miles per day on the Lost Coast. Second, there are only two stores on the entire route, in Petrolia and in Honeydew, so plan accordingly.

Ride

This epic ride begins as you leave the comforts of Highway 101 just south of Eureka, Calif. and ends as soon as you reach Highway 1, 31 miles north of Fort Bragg, Calif. To begin, exit Highway 101, 7 miles south of Eureka onto Eel River Road, following the signs to Loleta. The paved road climbs several hundred feet, and then drops into Loleta at **2.5 miles**. Continue along Eel River Road to an intersection with Highway 101, **4.5 miles**. Turn right, following the signs toward Fernbridge and Ferndale.

Reach Fernbridge, **5 miles**, and take a right, immediately crossing the Eel River on a narrow bridge. This is Highway 211. Arrive in Ferndale, a small town known for its well-preserved Victorian homes, at **9.5 miles**. Ferndale is the last town of any size for the following 130 miles, so stock up on supplies (though both Petrolia and Honeydew maintain small grocery stores).

Ride south on Main Street through Ferndale; just past the business district, the road bends to the right. Soon after this bend, turn left onto Mattole Road,

LOST COAST

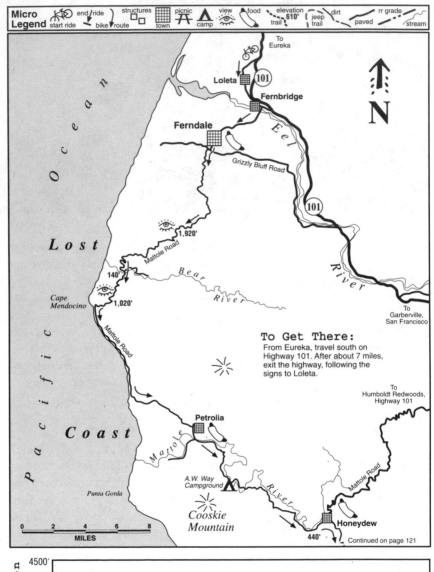

Micro Legend

start ride · end ride · bike route · structures · town · picnic · camp · view · food · elevation 610' · jeep trail · dirt · paved · rr grade · stream

To Eureka

Loleta · 101

Fernbridge

Ferndale

Grizzly Bluff Road

Eel River

101

Lost

Mattole Road

1,920'

140'

Cape Mendocino

1,020'

Bear River

To Garberville, San Francisco

Mattole Road

To Get There:
From Eureka, travel south on Highway 101. After about 7 miles, exit the highway, following the signs to Loleta.

To Humboldt Redwoods, Highway 101

Petrolia

Coast

Mattole River

A.W. Way Campground

Punta Gorda

Cooskie Mountain

Mattole Road

Honeydew

440'

N

Continued on page 121

| 0 | 2 | 4 | 6 | 8 |
MILES

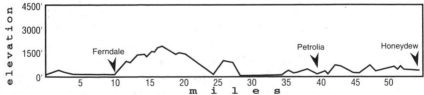

elevation (4500' 3000' 1500' 0')

Ferndale · Petrolia · Honeydew

miles — 5 10 15 20 25 30 35 40 45 50

LOST COAST

Continued from page 120

Micro Legend: end/ride, start ride, bike/route, structures, town, picnic, camp, view, food, elevation 610' trail, jeep trail, dirt, paved, rr grade, stream

Honeydew
440'
Mattole Rd.
To Eureka
Avenue of the Giants
101

King Range National Conservation Area

Mattole River
2,340'
Wilder Ridge Rd.
1,300'
Horse Mtn. Rd.
S. Fork
Thorne Road
Redway
Garberville

Ettersburg
Shelter Cove Rd.
Bear Cr.

Lost

2,100'
Shelter Cove
Point Delgada
Nadelos Campground
Wailaki Campground
1,320'
Chemise Mountain
Four Corners

Sinkyone
Jackass
Usal Road
Ridge

Wilderness
Usal Creek
101

Coast
Usal Road
1,980'
Leggett
To San Francisco

Usal Campground
40'
1
1,100'
To Fort Bragg

Pacific Ocean

N

0 2 4 6 8
MILES

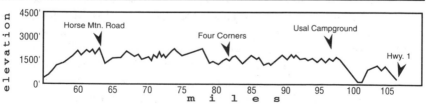

elevation				
4500'				
3000'	Horse Mtn. Road	Four Corners	Usal Campground	
1500'				Hwy. 1
0'				

60   65   70   75   80   85   90   95   100   105
m i l e s

Dirt road touring in the King Mountain Range

following the signs to Petrolia. The road, paved, but not much wider than one lane, immediately starts up a steep hill, providing a glimpse of the radical terrain to come. Other than a slight leveling at the **12-mile mark**, the road continues up at a feral grade to a ridge at **13.1 miles**.

From here, the road continues to climb the ridge through high grazing land and forested groves—though the way is peppered with short descents. Views from Bear River Ridge get better and better until, near the top at **17 miles**, the Eel River delta and Humboldt Bay are clearly visible to the north. Although it doesn't seem possible, Mattole Road narrows. After playing with the contours of the ridge in a gradual descent, the road switchbacks steeply down into Bear River Valley. Pass several farmhouses, then cross Bear River, **24.5 miles**.

Immediately after crossing the river, Mattole Road again heads up an arduous climb over Cape Ridge toward Cape Mendocino, the westernmost point in the continental United States. The road climbs nearly 1000 ft. in less than two miles, a very steep pitch. From the top, **26.2 miles**, survey the ocean views before abruptly dropping to the Pacific. **Whoa**, be careful of the severe switchbacks and steep grades. At **28.4 miles**, reach the ocean just south of Cape Mendocino. Pedal south, paralleling the rocky beach. This peaceful, flat stretch of Mattole Road is the last section of level riding on the Lost Coast, and the last section next to the Pacific Ocean until Usal Campground, six miles from the end of the ride.

At **34.5 miles**, the road bends to the left, away from the ocean. The road is steep at first, but then ascends gradually to a high point at **27.6 miles**. From this point, drop down toward the little town of Petrolia. At **39.5 miles**, pass the store in Petrolia, one of two on the Lost Coast. Through the tiny, spread-out town, stay on Mattole Road, which makes a weird switchback just past the store. At **40.5 miles,** reach a fork in the road, after crossing the Mattole River. Take the left fork, following the signs for Honeydew and staying on Mattole Road.

The road, which is still paved, parallels the Mattole River for a short time, then cuts away and climbs abruptly. Earn the top at **43 miles,** then descend—gradually at first, then quickly back to the river. At **46 miles,** pass A.W. Way Campground on the right, which is tucked into a bend in the Mattole River. From the campground, the road climbs, for the most part, winding along the south bank of the Mattole River.

Though Mattole Road since Ferndale has been narrow, lacking a yellow line and shoulder to mark the edge of the road, few cars drive the route. At **54.2 miles,** arrive at the hamlet of Honeydew, and the last store on the route, which is open seven days a week during the summer. The road divides in Honeydew: turn right onto Wilder Ridge Road (Mattole Road, left, travels back to Highway 101, 23 miles). Wilder Ridge Road, a paved road with neither yellow lines nor a white centerline, follows Honeydew Creek for a short stretch.

At **56.1 miles,** the road crosses a creek and turns to dirt. Immediately the road becomes so steep that every cyclist will consider turning back. The dirt road climbs to a fork at **57 miles**—go left. At **57.3 miles,** pass a road on the left and continue up. Reach a false summit as the road gains the top edge of Wilder Ridge at **58.4 miles.** From here, the road crests a series of illusory summits as the ridge rises into the King Mountain Range. With the ride from Honeydew up Wilder Ridge, this Lost Coast ride begins to reveal its full intensity.

At **63 miles,** the road divides at the top of the ridge. The road, which has been paved in a couple of short sections, is now paved. **Whoa,** to continue the ride, abandon the pavement and turn right onto Horse Mountain Road (called Kings Peak Road on some maps), which is gravel (the paved, right-hand fork leads to Ettersburg and, eventually, Highway 101). After the fork, the rough and rutted dirt road immediately switchbacks precipitously downward, losing over 1,000 ft. in less than a mile. The jolting descent complete, the road crosses the North Fork of Bear Creek, **63.9 miles,** and begins climbing.

For the next fifteen miles, the road more or less parallels the South Fork of Bear Creek, although the creek is usually hidden deep in the valley. Bear scat litters the road over the next several miles, validating the name of the drainage. After a short, steep pitch, the climb is more moderate. At **65 miles,** arrive at a T, turn left, staying on the main route. From the turn, the road rollercoasters to a summit of sorts at **67.3 miles.** Pass Horse Mountain Campground on the left, **68 miles.** At a fork in the road just past the campground, turn left and continue downhill. After more tough ups and downs, pass Tolkan Campground on the left. After the campground, stay on the main road as it climbs over several significant hills. Reach a paved road at a T, **74.5 miles.**

From the pavement, turn left onto Shelter Cove Road (the community of

*Descending the
Usal Road toward
Highway 1*

Shelter Cove is four miles to the right; Redway and Highway 101 are 19 miles to the left). Pedal one-half mile on the paved road toward Redway, and turn right onto Chemise Mountain Road, which immediately becomes dirt, **75 miles**. Pass Nadelos Campground at **76.6 miles** and then Wailaki Campground at **77 miles**. Just past the two campgrounds, the road climbs over a summit, **77.8 miles**, leaving the South Fork of Bear Creek drainage. From the top, the road descends precipitously for a time, then rollercoasters.

Pass a tiny trailer village at **80.4 miles**. At **81.6 miles**, arrive at a 4-way intersection called Four Corners. Continue straight through the intersection. Chemise Mountain Road becomes Usal Road. The road, only one-lane wide, climbs up Jackass Ridge and rides along the top edge of it through madrone and oak forests. **Whoa**, avoid this section during wet weather because the road has a high clay content which could compromise traction. After a series of steep climbs and descents, pass over the high point of Usal Road, **91 miles**.

Jackass Ridge affords some amazing views of the ocean and of the jagged coastal mountains. From the high point, the road gradually descends to **94.8 miles**. The road heads uphill again, mounting Timber Ridge. Just prior to the top of the ridge, pass a gated road on the right that leads to the old ghost town of Wheeler. From the top, Usal Road drops toward Usal Creek; beginning at **98.3 miles**, it makes a dive-bomb descent to Usal Campground and the Pacific Ocean.

Reach Usal Campground, and sea level, at **101.2 miles**. From the campground, follow the main road to the base of the next climb. The dirt road south of Usal Campground ascends straight up over the headland. Most of the serious climbing is complete at **103.2 miles**, although the road doesn't top out until **105.2 miles**. All along this stretch, waves crash against the rocks below the headland, views of the coastline extend north and south. From the top, Usal Road descends quickly to Highway 1 between Leggett and Westport. At **107 miles**, the ride ends.

RUSSIAN GULCH BIKE & HIKE

Checklist: 4.2 miles, Out & Back; dirt trail, paved trail
Duration: 1 hour
Hill factor: easy upward grade
Skill level: beginner
Map: *Jackson State Forest*, California Dept. of Forestry
Season: spring, summer, fall
User density: high; cyclists, walkers, wheelchairs
Explorability: low

Teaser

The trail from Russian Gulch Campground winds gently upward along a delicate creek. The banks are covered with ferns and poison oak. The multi-use section of the path, wide and well-surfaced, ends at a few picnic tables at a bend in the creek. From here, the trails are pedestrian only, but the walk up to the small, picturesque falls is beautiful. Given the wide, mostly paved trail, this rates as a one-wheel ride. Be courteous of other users on the ride back to the campground.

Waterfall near the end of Russian Gulch

RUSSIAN GULCH BIKE & HIKE

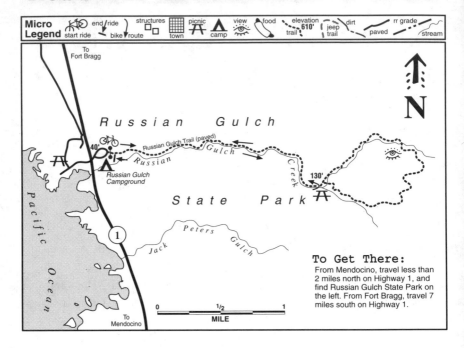

Micro Legend: end/ride, start ride, bike route, structures, town, picnic, camp, view, food, elevation 610', trail, jeep trail, dirt, paved, rr grade, stream

To Fort Bragg

N

Russian Gulch

40' — Russian Gulch Trail (paved) — Gulch

Russian

Russian Gulch Campground

Creek

130'

State Park

Peters Gulch

Jack Gulch

1

Pacific Ocean

To Get There:
From Mendocino, travel less than 2 miles north on Highway 1, and find Russian Gulch State Park on the left. From Fort Bragg, travel 7 miles south on Highway 1.

0   1/2   1
MILE

To Mendocino

Ride

From the entrance booth of Russian Gulch State Park, drop down the steep hill into the campground. Angling east, wind through campsites for **.5 mile** to a gate. The Fern Canyon Trail begins at the gate; a sign is posted there prohibiting fast riding.

Six-feet-wide and sometimes paved, the trail follows a sweet little creek. Opposite the creek, the wet banks of Fern Canyon rise, lush with ferns, poison oak, salal, cedar, redwood, and douglas fir. The trail, covered with pine needles and some mud, climbs gradually. At **2.1 miles**, the pavement ends for good at a tiny picnic area. This is the end of the trail for bicycles. Retrace your steps to the campground, **4.2 miles**.

If you continue by foot to the falls (highly recommended), the trail climbs at a more difficult rate, and the trail is much narrower. The trail divides immediately after the picnic area. The left fork reaches the waterfall .7 mile further; the right trail reaches the waterfall 2.3 miles from the picnic area.

JACKSON STATE FOREST ❀❀❀

Checklist: 17.7 miles, Loop; dirt roads, jeep trails, paved roads
Duration: 3–4 hours
Hill factor: long climbs, some steep sections
Skill level: intermediate
Map: *Jackson State Forest*, California Dept. of Forestry
Season: spring, summer, fall
User density: low; cyclists, walkers, hunters, vehicles
Explorability: high

Teaser

Fort Bragg, originally established as an outpost to keep coastal Indians out of prime timberland, became the logging hub of northern California around the beginning of the twentieth century. Although much of the town's logging industry has closed, the 52,000-acre Jackson State Forest remains a working forest, laced with many miles of logging roads. Some, like many of the roads on this ride through the Caspar Creek Watershed, are no longer used by logging trucks; other roads still provide thoroughfare to cut timber. This ride is located primarily on dirt roads, some of which have been gated to motor vehicles. The roads are, for the most part, non-technical, but some of the climbs are long. This hill factor combined with the distance make it a three-wheel excursion. The lushness of the forest and the detail of the Jackson State Forest topographic map beckon any mountain biker with a taste for exploring—this is your bliss (as long as you can ignore the recreational shooting off in the distance).

Ride

Beginning from the intersection of Highway 1 and Fern Creek Road, ride east. Climb to Caspar Orchard Road, **.3 mile**, and turn right. At **.5 mile**, Caspar Orchard Road, which is paved, turns to the left. Take the right fork, the Caspar Logging Road (Road 500 on the map), which is dirt. At **1.5 miles**, roads exit in every direction; keep a cool head and turn right onto Road 600. This road, which gets some traffic, drops down to the cooler, darker forests next to Caspar Creek.

At **3.8 miles**, find the Caspar Creek Cooperative Watershed Study sign at a 4-way intersection. Take the road on the right, Road 600, that gradually climbs, rougher and narrower, away from the intersection. Take the right fork at **4 miles**.

(At 4.5 miles, the left fork rejoins the main road.) After a descent, the road rises again, then drops to a sign: "Road closed, bridge unsafe."

At **5.1 miles**, cross the short bridge—it appears safe for bicycles—and start climbing. The road rises and falls to a left-hand hairpin bend in the road at the **6.4-mile mark**. Afterward, climb steadily to a T at **6.8 miles**. (The left fork returns to the 4-way intersection at 3.8 miles.) Take the right fork which continues the relentless ascent. Stay on main road: small trails and lesser roads off the main road are prevalent. After a stiff climb, crest the hill at **8.3 miles**. At **8.5 miles**, reach a T at Mendocino County Road 408.

Turn left onto Road 408 which, though dirt, is heavily trafficked. As the road rolls up and down, pass several lesser roads on the right and left—stay on the main road. At **9.2 miles**, turn right onto Road 630, a gated jeep trail. **Whoa**, it cuts back to the left and could be easily missed. As the road descends, pass two gated roads on the right at **9.4 and 10.1 miles**. At **11.9 miles**, after a long, fast downhill, the jeep trail finally levels out and actually climbs slightly.

At **13.9 miles**, pass a gate just before a fork in the jeep trail—take the downhill fork to the right. The route returns to the 4-way intersection at **14.3 miles**. From here, pedal back to Highway 1 via Road 600, Road 500, Caspar Orchard Road, and Fern Creek Road to complete the ride, **17.7 miles**.

JACKSON STATE FOREST

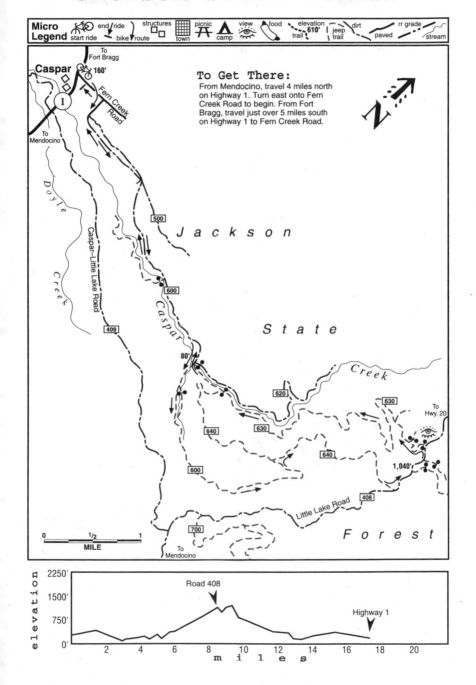

Micro Legend — end/ride, start ride, bike route, structures, town, picnic, camp, view, food, elevation 610' trail, jeep trail, dirt, paved, rr grade, stream

To Get There:
From Mendocino, travel 4 miles north on Highway 1. Turn east onto Fern Creek Road to begin. From Fort Bragg, travel just over 5 miles south on Highway 1 to Fern Creek Road.

To Fort Bragg

Caspar 160'

1

To Mendocino

Fern Creek Road

Doyle Creek

Caspar–Little Lake Road

Caspar Creek

Jackson   State   Creek   Forest

500
600
80'
409
620
630
640
630
640
600
408
700

To Hwy. 20

1,040'

Little Lake Road

To Mendocino

0   1/2   1
MILE

elevation (2250', 1500', 750', 0')

Road 408

Highway 1

miles (2, 4, 6, 8, 10, 12, 14, 16, 18, 20)

PYGMY FOREST ✸✸✸

Checklist: 9.5 miles, Loop; dirt trails, dirt roads, paved road
Duration: 2–3 hours
Hill factor: some moderate climbing
Skill level: advanced
Map: *Jackson State Forest*, California Dept. of Forestry
Season: spring, summer, fall
User density: moderate; cyclists, walkers
Explorability: moderate

Teaser

This ride begins and ends in Mendocino, a small tourist and art community built onto a small piece of rock above the Pacific. The ride climbs up a paved road to a single-track trail that winds through an unusual pygmy forest. These forests, named for the stunted and gnarled trees, developed over many centuries due to a combination of acidic soil and extreme water conditions. While you ride, watch for knotted, three-foot pines and cypress which may be as much as one hundred years old. *Catch A Canoe and Bicycles, Too*, the bicycle shop located just across Big River from Mendocino, only recommends this ride for Sundays because logging trucks use the dirt road which comes at the end of the ride. Be careful.

Riding the dirt road along Big River

PYGMY FOREST

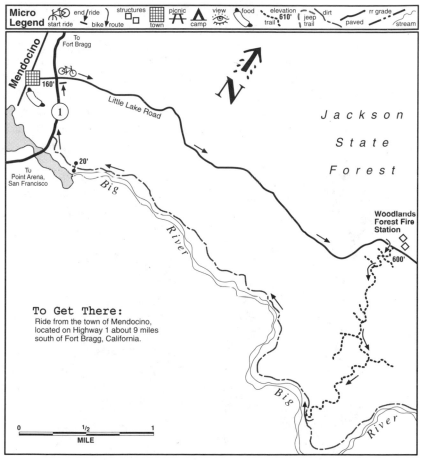

Micro Legend
end/ride — structures — picnic — town — picnic camp — view — food — elevation 610' trail — jeep trail dirt — rr grade — paved — stream
start ride — bike route

To Fort Bragg

Mendocino

160'

1

To Point Arena, San Francisco

20'

Little Lake Road

Big River

J a c k s o n
S t a t e
F o r e s t

Woodlands Forest Fire Station
600'

To Get There:
Ride from the town of Mendocino, located on Highway 1 about 9 miles south of Fort Bragg, California.

Big River

0   1/2   1
MILE

elevation
1800'
1200'
600'
0'
Mendocino   pygmy forest   Big River
2   4   6   8   10
m i l e s

Ride

From the intersection of Highway 1 and Little Lake Road just across from Mendocino, pedal out Little Lake Road. For the first **.6 mile**, follow the bike lane. The lane ends at the Mendocino grammar school. At **3.1 miles**, right across the street from Woodlands Forest Fire Station, find a narrow trail on the right.

Turn right off the road onto the trail. The trail winds through the stunted forests, past numerous lesser trails, to a T at **4.3 miles**. Be sure to stay on the main trail. At the T, turn left onto a jeep trail. The jeep trail narrows a bit, before reaching a fork at **4.6 miles**. Take the right fork (actually straight) and continue down the hill.

At **5.2 miles**, drop to the road that runs along Big River—the North Big River Road. Turn right (west) and pedal down river. Be careful, this is a heavily used logging road, and there may be trucks on it. At **8.5 miles**, reach a gate. Pass a beach on the river, left, and at **9.0 miles**, bear right and climb up to the end of North Big River Road which intersects with Highway 1, south of Mendocino. Turn right and ride up to the stop light at Little Lake Road to finish the loop, **9.5 miles**.

Single track through a pygmy forest

MORE RIDES

Crescent City

In addition to the rides detailed here, there are numerous mountain bicycle opportunities on dirt roads and trails near Crescent City, Calif. The best resources are *Redwood National Park*, a map published by Trails Illustrated, and *The Hiker's Hip Pocket Guide to the Humboldt Coast* by Bob Lorentzen, published by Bored Feet Publications.

Fort Bragg Haul Road

From MacKerricher State Park Campground north of Fort Bragg, Calif., ride down toward the ocean and around Lake Cleone. Locate the old Haul Road, which cuts across the bluffs just above the Pacific toward Fort Bragg. Pass under the Haul Road, then immediately turn left to access it. This flat, paved, non-motorized road is about 3.5 miles long. This is an easy beginner ride and a pleasant alternative touring route to Highway 1.

Humboldt Redwoods

Beyond the two rides in Humboldt Redwoods State Park already described, many other fire roads criss-cross the park. While the routes available to bicycles are generally on dirt roads, most of these routes are extremely difficult due to huge elevation gains. The best resource is a map from the California Department of Parks & Recreation, *Humboldt Redwoods State Park*. For more information, call ☎ 707-946-2409.

Jackson State Forest

Two rides in Jackson State Forest are included in *Wild Pigs*. But this state forest spreads out over 50,000 acres, so there are many, many more miles of dirt roads and trails available to the mountain-bike explorer. For more information, call the forest headquarters, ☎ 707-964-5674.

TO THE
SAN FRANCISCO
BAY AREA

PRELUDE

By candlelight in the hiker/biker site at Manchester Beach Campground, I learned to tie a balloon into a tiger. "Pinch, double twist, fold over, then double twist again," it was explained as I twisted and pinched. Even after several starts, my blue tiger ended up lopsided and out of proportion, one ear larger than the other, his head about twice the size of his puny body.

We had heard stories of a "balloon man" cycling the coast. He financed his trip by selling balloon tigers and Mickey Mouses and even bicycles as he traveled. He was waiting in Leggett, of all places, for his next shipment of special balloons. It seemed a little far-fetched. But Dwain became real when we rolled up next to him on Highway 1 about one mile north of Manchester Beach and got a glimpse of his enormous handlebar bag of colored balloons. Dwain had been touring for over a year, selling his rubber creations to, well, anyone who would buy one. After we lent him a spoke wrench, he offered to teach us how to tie a tiger.

Despite the proportions of my tiger, I thanked Dwain for the lesson. The next morning after breakfast, I attached my little tiger to the top of my sleeping bag just behind my seat. I glided south, winding and rollercoasting past Point Arena and Gualala and Fort Ross. My tiger held on tight, even on the dramatic switchbacking descent near the Russian River.

The day ended 25 miles north of San Francisco at Samuel P. Taylor Park. The next few days would be mountain biking at Point Reyes (page 142) and on the infamous Mount Tamalpais (pages 147 and 150) before continuing along the bustling streets into and through San Francisco.

Though my little blue tiger had toured with me so peacefully, flapping slightly on the fast downhills, sitting patiently on the slow uphills, watching over the bikes while I bought lunch at a grocery in Valley Ford, he had bumped against my tire a few too many times. His huge head was smudged. It occurred to me that riding on the back of the bike and scuffing his head was a bit undignified for a tiger, so I put him on top of the front rack like a hood ornament. And after a few days of great mountain biking, the tiger and I continued touring south. He seemed much happier.

TOUR GUIDE

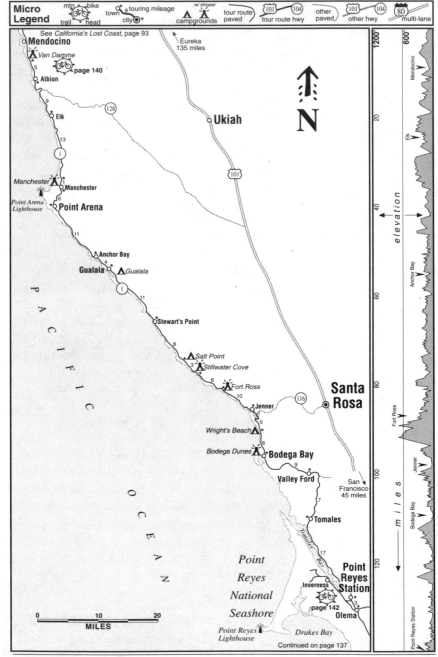

Micro Legend — mtn bike / trail / head / town / city / 8 touring mileage / w/ shower campgrounds / tour route paved / tour route hwy / other paved / other hwy / multi-lane

See *California's Lost Coast*, page 93

Mendocino
Van Damme
5
Albion — page 140
9
Elk
13
I
128
Ukiah
101

N

Manchester — **Manchester**
6
Point Arena Lighthouse — **Point Arena**
11

Anchor Bay
4
Gualala — Gualala
I
11

Stewart's Point
8
Salt Point
3 — Stillwater Cove
6 — Fort Ross
10
Jenner
116
Santa Rosa
5
Wright's Beach
6
Bodega Dunes — **Bodega Bay**
9
Valley Ford
7
San Francisco 45 miles
Tomales

Eureka 135 miles

PACIFIC OCEAN

17
Point Reyes National Seashore
Inverness
6
Point Reyes Station
page 142
3
Olema
Point Reyes Lighthouse — *Drakes Bay*

0   10   20
MILES

elevation — miles

1200' / 600'
Mendocino
20
Elk
40
Anchor Bay
60
Fort Ross
80
Jenner
Bodega Bay
100
120
Point Reyes Station

Continued on page 137

TOUR GUIDE

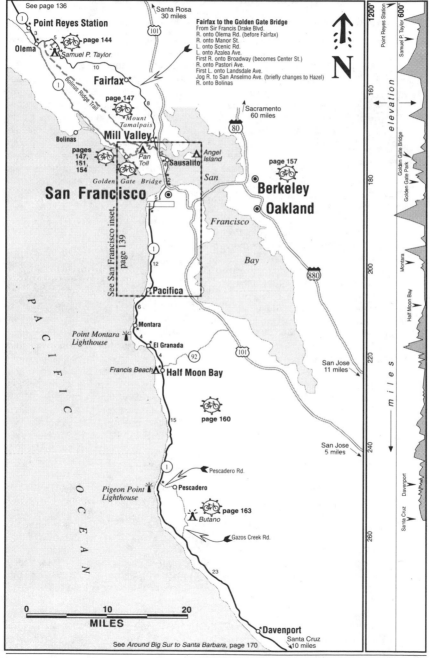

See page 136

Point Reyes Station

Olema

page 144

Samuel P. Taylor

Santa Rosa
30 miles

Fairfax

Fairfax to the Golden Gate Bridge
From Sir Francis Drake Blvd.
R. onto Olema Rd. (before Fairfax)
R. onto Manor St.
L. onto Scenic Rd.
L. onto Azalea Ave.
First R. onto Broadway (becomes Center St.)
R. onto Pastori Ave.
First L. onto Landsdale Ave.
Jog R. to San Anselmo Ave. (briefly changes to Hazel)
R. onto Bolinas

N

page 147

Mount
Tamalpais

Mill Valley

Bolinas

pages
147,
151,
154

Pan
Toll

Sausalito

Angel
Island

San

page 157

Berkeley

Golden Gate Bridge

San Francisco

Oakland

Francisco

Bay

See San Francisco inset,
page 139

Pacifica

Sacramento
60 miles

Montara

Point Montara
Lighthouse

El Granada

Francis Beach

Half Moon Bay

San Jose
11 miles

San Jose
5 miles

page 160

Pescadero Rd.

Pigeon Point
Lighthouse

Pescadero

page 163

Butano

Gazos Creek Rd.

P A C I F I C   O C E A N

Davenport

Santa Cruz
10 miles

0   10   20
MILES

See *Around Big Sur to Santa Barbara*, page 170

elevation

Point Reyes Station

Samuel P. Taylor

Golden Gate Bridge

Golden Gate Park

Montara

Half Moon Bay

Santa Cruz

Davenport

m i l e s

160

180

200

220

240

260

1200'

600'

QUICK FACTS

miles (touring south from Mendocino, CA)

0   **SEE:** The little town of **Mendocino** sits

on a rocky headland above the crashing waves of the Pacific. You'll find a great bakery with a grocery next door. Around the corner, find perhaps the only bookstore between Arcata and San Francisco that sells *The New Yorker.*

0   **READ:** Bob Lorentzen writes a series of trail guides for all types of users, including mountain bikers. So *The Hiker's Hip Pocket Guide to the Mendocino Coast* contains numerous trails for two-wheel tripping.

0   **RIDE:** If you plan to do any riding in **Jackson State Forest** (page 140), the large topo map is a fine investment. Find miles of dirt roads, many gated to motor vehicles, throughout the forest.

1   **REPAIR & SLEEP:** Across the Big River from Mendocino, find **Catch A Canoe & Bicycles, Too**, ☎ 707-937-0273, a helpful and well-equipped bike shop that also rents canoes. Lots of helpful information about riding in the Jackson State Forest. If the mountain biking was too tough, just up the driveway, find **The Stanford Inn by the Sea**, ☎ 800-331-8884, a B&B which has an expansive herb garden, llamas, and an indoor pool and spa. Reservations required well in advance.

1   **SLEEP:** Can't find a room? Try the **California Association of Bed & Breakfast Inns**, ☎ 800-284-4667.

2   **CAMP:** Use **Van Damme Campground**, or **Russian Gulch** just north of Mendocino, as a base camp for mountain biking in Jackson State Forest (page 127), the pygmy forest (page 130), and Fern Canyon (page 140).

140 **EAT:** Stop by the **Bovine Bakery** on the main drag in Point Reyes Station to satisfy that pastry craving.

miles (touring south from Mendocino, CA)

145* **SLEEP:** Just north of Inverness on the Point Reyes peninsula, find the **Sandy Cove Inn**, ☎ 800-759-2683. A beautiful and secluded home that looks east across Tomales Bay, the property boasts the largest eucalyptus tree in Marin County. The innkeepers, Kathy and Gerry Coles, prove that trail-use wars are misguided. Kathy, an avid equestrian, and Gerry, a committed mountain bicyclist, ride together on trails throughout Marin. Whatever your call-

ing—hiking, cycling, riding a horse, bird watching, eating—they will recommend the best places. Of course you can always just lounge on the beach and watch the sailboats float across Tomales Bay after a superb breakfast. Massages are available for both beach loungers and mountain bicyclists.

145 **INFORMATION & RIDE:** Bear Val-

ley Visitor's Center, ☎ 415-663-1092, is the park headquarters for Point Reyes National Seashore. The center provides lots of pertinent information on trails, camping, lighthouses, history, and more. The Bear Valley mountain bike ride begins here (page 142).

150 **CAMP:** Discover more ancient redwoods at **Samuel P. Taylor State Park**, ☎ 415-488-9897. While touring this is almost a mandatory stop since it is the

last campground before San Francisco (Half Moon Bay is the next). It makes a nice base camp for mountain biking on Bolinas Ridge, Point Reyes, and Mount Tamalpais.

170* **SLEEP:** Near the top of Panoramic Hwy. on the way to Stinson Beach, find the **Mountain Home Inn,** ☎ 415-381-9000. Not quite as personal as other B&Bs, the Mountain Home Inn is the perfect base camp for a ride up Mount Tam. Many of the rooms provide incredible views east toward the Berkeley Hills; on clear nights, Orion rises over the lights of the Bay Bridge. The entry to the inn is dramatic with raw logs used as columns. Some rooms have jacuzzis for those tired, Hoo-Koo-E-Koo muscles.

165 **INSET: San Francisco.**

170* **CAMP:** Just a few miles west from Mountain Home Inn on Panoramic Hwy., find **Pantoll Campground** ☎ 415-388-2070. This primitive, 16-site campground doubles as the trailhead for many Mount Tamalpais rides (see pages 147, 151). If you are touring,

miles (touring south from Mendocino, CA)

reaching Pantoll is problematic: Panoramic Hwy. is steep, winding, and dangerous for loaded tourists. Adventurers can ride the Bolinas Ridge Trail (dirt) from Samuel P. Taylor Park. This trail connects with West Ridgecrest Blvd. (paved) and leads to Pantoll.

170* **READ:** When riding on Mount Tam, perhaps the best known mountain bike spot on earth after Moab, the Olmsted & Bros. map is mandatory. Most bike shops carry **Trails of Mt. Tamalpais and the Marin Headland.**

175 **READ: Mountain Biking in the Bay Area** by Michael Hodgson and Mark Lord is the mountain bike guide for the region. Unfortunately, this 210-page guidebook contains just six photos, including a shot of the authors.

182 **SEE:** In the midst of civilized **Golden Gate Park**, pass by some very non-civilized wild beasts—the park's buffalo herd. Stop for a moment to check out their huge heads and thick tongues.

210 **READ:** Krebs Cycle Products publishes a wonderful map—**Mountain Biking Map: San Francisco Peninsula and Santa Cruz Mountains.** Described on the front cover as "the world's best," this map is full of creative innovations that provide much fun and instruction both on the trail and at home.

215* **RIDE: Purisima Creek Redwoods Open Space** (page 160)—nice single track just south of San Francisco.

235* **CAMP & RIDE:** Just slightly off the touring route, find **Butano State Park,** ☎ 415-879-2040. Leave the open, coastal grasslands for lush redwood forests, with banana slugs, mushrooms, newts, and a determined band of raccoons. Mountain bike from the campground (page 163).

*indicates site off tour route

FERN CANYON ⊛⊛

Checklist: 8.3 miles, Loop; dirt roads, paved road
Duration: 1–2 hours
Hill factor: some moderate climbing on paved road
Skill level: intermediate
Map: *Jackson State Forest*, California Dept. of Forestry
Season: spring, summer, fall
User density: high; cyclists, walkers
Explorability: low

Teaser

Like the ride on page 130 which travels through a section of pygmy forest, the Fern Canyon ride also passes by this northern California coastal oddity. In the

ride along Little River in Fern Canyon, layers of ferns and the rushing sound of the river make for a hypnotic and magical experience. This easy ride, nearly half of it on pavement, is a nice excursion for the family, or anyone staying at Van Damme Campground. The only difficult section, a steep descent from a pygmy forest grove to Little River, mandates a two-wheel rating.

*Lush growth along Little River,
Van Damme Beach State Park*

FERN CANYON

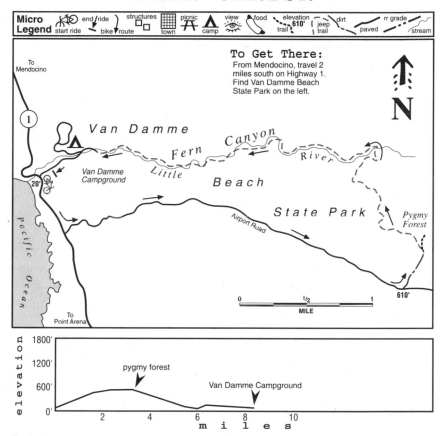

Ride

From the entrance of Van Damme Campground, pedal south on Highway 1. The highway climbs slightly away from the beach. At **.6 mile**, turn left onto Little River Airport Road. This road climbs steadily as it heads east toward the airport.

Pass the small Mendocino County Airport at **2.8 miles**. At **3.5 miles**, turn left into the Pygmy Forest parking area. Locate the trailhead for the gated dirt road that leads back to the campground at **3.7 miles**. A pedestrian-only interpretive trail through the pygmy forest also leaves from the same trailhead.

On the way back to Van Damme, stay on the main road—wide, hard-pack dirt—as it switchbacks down to Little River. Ferns cover the forest floor like a low fog; redwood and fir stand tall above the melee. At **5.2 miles**, climb to an abandoned parking area. At **5.7 miles**, pass through an environmental camp.

After crossing Little River several times, pass through Van Damme Campground at **7.7 miles**. Reach Highway 1 to complete the loop, **8.3 miles**.

BEAR VALLEY BIKE & HIKE ✸

Checklist: 8.4 miles, Out & Back; jeep trail, dirt trail
Duration: 1–2 hours
Hill factor: easy climb
Skill level: beginner
Map: *Point Reyes*, National Park Service
Season: spring, summer, fall
User density: high; cyclists, walkers, equestrians
Explorability: low

Teaser

The Bear Valley Bike & Hike is an easy ride for those unsure about mountain bikes or their own fitness. It is also just a lovely ride that any bicyclist will enjoy. The wide, smooth hard-packed dirt road affords easy pedaling. But despite the easy nature of the ride, Point Reyes is a wild place. Rocky cliffs and dangerous tides, bobcats, tics, and swarms of ladybugs, poison oak and unpredictable weather year-round all make this a place to honor. It's amazing that a place like this can be located so close to a huge city like San Francisco.

Ride

Starting from the parking lot of the visitor center at Point Reyes, pedal out the wide, dirt Bear Valley Trail. As the trail gradually climbs, pass by a trail on the right and then another on the left. Large oak and cypress are scattered across the grassy fields.

Pedal across the top of a small rise, **.6 mile**. At the same time, pass Divide Meadow picnic area on the left and another no-bikes trailhead. Continue down Bear Valley Trail, descending now. The woods are thicker now, brimming with, among other things, poison oak. At **3.2 miles**, reach a 4-way intersection. This is the Phillip Burton Wilderness boundary and the end of the bicycle route; it is marked with a bicycle rack. From here, bikes are precluded from all three trails.

To see the Pacific, leave your bike at the rack and walk down to Arch Rock, about 1 mile further. (If you do not have a lock, carry your front wheel with you to the water. Though technically, that may be against the rules, too.) Retrace your steps to the visitor's center. Including the hike to Arch Rock, the total distance comes to **8.4-miles**.

BEAR VALLEY BIKE & HIKE

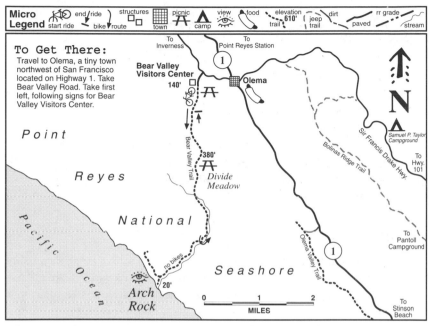

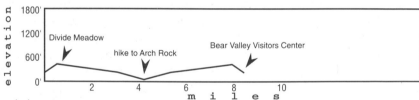

Exploring Arch Rock at Point Reyes

DEVILS GULCH ✸✸✸

Checklist: 4.7 miles, Loop; dirt roads, dirt trails, paved roads
Duration: 1–2 hours
Hill factor: steep grades, several pushes
Skill level: advanced
Map: *Samuel P. Taylor Park*, California State Parks
Season: spring, summer, fall
User density: high; cyclists, walkers, equestrians
Explorability: moderate

Teaser

The Devils Gulch ride graphically presents the problem of rating mountain-bike rides. While nearly half of the 4.7-mile route travels on wide, flat roads and trails, there is a series of hills on the other half of the ride that are so steep that most riders will have to walk up and down them. It's a two-wheel ride as far as the distance and riding surface go; a four-wheel ride as far as the hills go. I've managed the inelegant writer's compromise and rated it three wheels. Other trails in Samuel P. Taylor Park are open to bicycles, although climber's thighs are recommended. The bicycle trail that passes through the campground also leads to other rides outside the park, including the Bolinas Ridge Trail.

Ride

Start at the entrance to the Samuel P. Taylor Campground and Sir Francis Drake Highway. Turn left onto Sir Francis Drake Highway, toward Olema. Pass by the Madrone Group Camp at **.3 mile**. The Devils Gulch Trailhead exits to the right at a gate, **1 mile**. Take this right turn and pedal up the paved road.

Pass several horse camps at **1.2 miles**. At this point find the trail on the right and take it, **1.3 miles**. (If you continue straight, the road turns to dirt and then climbs to a gate 1.2 miles further.) The trail, narrow and dirt, drops to a bridge. Across Devils Gulch Creek bear right and immediately begin a stiff climb. At **1.5 miles**, the way divides. Take the bike trail, which continues a difficult climb around to the left, toward a large U-shaped section of trail.

The trail climbs to a high point, which is also the bottom of the U, and sweeps to the right, **1.7 miles**. At **1.9 miles**, after a very steep downhill, arrive at a 4-way intersection. Take the center route, again climbing. The trail reaches the Barnabe

DEVILS GULCH

Micro Legend: start ride / end ride · bike / route · structures · town · picnic · camp · view · food · elevation 610' · trail / jeep trail · dirt / paved · rr grade · stream

To Get There:
From San Rafael, travel south on Highway 101. Go west on Sir Francis Drake Blvd, past Fairfax, to Samuel P. Taylor State Park.

Gulch Creek

Devils

Samuel P. Taylor

State Park

no bikes

440'

140'

Lagunitas

Creek

Sir Francis Drake Blvd.

To Olema, Hwy. 1

To Bolinas Trail

To San Rafael, Hwy. 101

Samuel P. Taylor Campground

0   1/4   1/2
MILE

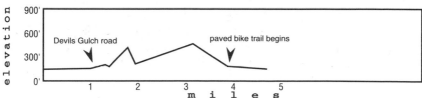

elevation

900'
600'
300'
0'

Devils Gulch road

paved bike trail begins

1   2   3   4   5
miles

Bridge across Devils Gulch Creek, Samuel P. Taylor State Park

Trail at a T—turn uphill to the left. After a short uphill pitch, the trail divides—turn right. The trail traverses, dropping slightly, toward Barnabe Creek.

When the trail forks at **3.1 miles**, stay left and continue traversing. At **3.4 miles**, just past an old water tower, the trail veers to the right and descends precipitously. Just before the trail reaches Sir Francis Drake Highway, turn left onto a narrow trail, **3.5 miles. Whoa**, this is an easy turn to miss. This narrow trail meets a bicycle trail at **3.8 miles**.

Turn right and pedal over a bridge that crosses Sir Francis Drake Highway. Ride along the wide, sporadically paved trail until it reaches Samuel P. Taylor Campground, **4.4 miles**. Follow the signs to the park entrance to complete the loop, **4.7 miles**.

HOO-KOO-E-KOO ✿✿✿✿

Checklist: 12.6 miles, Loop; dirt road, 1 mile paved
Duration: 2–4 hours
Hill factor: some steep climbs, several pushes
Skill level: intermediate
Map: *Trails of Mt. Tamalpais*, Olmsted & Bros. Map Co.
Season: year round
User density: medium; cyclists, walkers, equestrians
Explorability: high

Teaser

Often referred to as the birthplace of modern mountain biking, Mount Tamalpais—known everywhere as Mount Tam—is covered with beautiful and challenging dirt roads and trails. Regrettably, Mount Tam is also known as the site of the mother of all trail-use battles, and mountain bicyclists have been tossed from nearly all the single-track trails on the mountain. (Some local riders, using strong, 16-watt lighting systems, ride the trails at night when rangers and other users aren't likely to be out on the trails.) But despite the restrictions and

Views of San Francisco Bay from Mount Tamalpais

Riding on Mount Tamalpais

animosity between user groups, Mount Tamalpais remains a great place to ride, with dozens of dirt roads to choose from. This particular route is one of the classic Mount Tam rides; it includes the Hoo-Koo-E-Koo trail made famous by Fisher Bicycles; the West Point Inn, a train stop during the golden days of the old "Gravity Car" railroad; and the summit of the East Peak of Mount Tam. Be sure to obey the posted regulations which include a 15-mph speed limit. Oh yeah, and if anyone spots a wild pig while cycling on Mount Tam, you are asked by the rangers to report it. But don't you think you should give that a second thought?

Ride

Begin from the Pantoll Campground near the top of the Panoramic Highway. Across the highway from the campground, there are two paved roads that head north. Take the road on the right and begin climbing. When the road forks, take the left fork onto a dirt road, the Old Stage Road.

Pass through a gate, **.6 mile**. At **2.6 miles**, reach West Point Inn, a place bikers, hikers, and equestrians can stop for a lemonade on a hot day. Early this century, the West Point Inn was a stop on the "Gravity Car" railroad on its way to the top of Mount Tamalpais. Indeed, from the inn bear to the right to access the Old Railroad Grade Trail, now a dirt road, and begin descending. During the entire downward traverse across the south flank of Mount Tam, the Old Railroad Grade Trail affords awesome views of San Francisco and the bay.

At **3.9 miles**, reach the famous Hoo-Koo-E-Koo Trail and make a hard left-hand turn. **Whoa**, this is an easy turn to miss. The Hoo-Koo-E-Koo Trail, a dirt

HOO-KOO-E-KOO

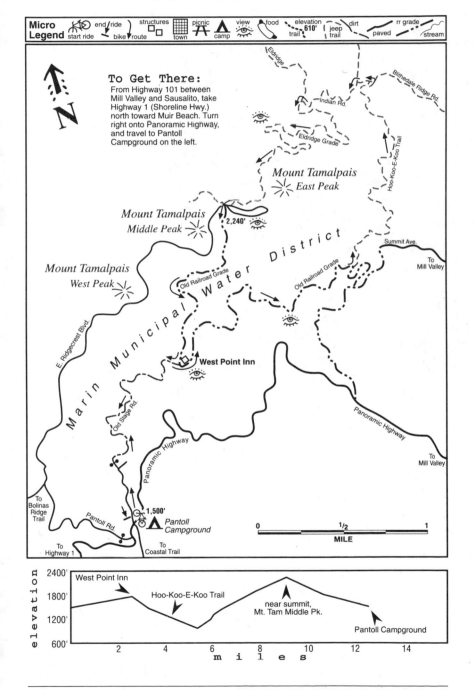

Micro Legend: end ride, start ride, bike route, structures, town, picnic, camp, view, food, elevation 610', trail, dirt, jeep trail, rr grade, paved, stream

To Get There:
From Highway 101 between Mill Valley and Sausalito, take Highway 1 (Shoreline Hwy.) north toward Muir Beach. Turn right onto Panoramic Highway, and travel to Pantoll Campground on the left.

N

Eldridge

Blithedale Ridge Rd.

Indian Rd.

Eldridge Grade

Hoo-Koo-E-Koo Trail

Mount Tamalpais East Peak

Mount Tamalpais Middle Peak

2,240'

Mount Tamalpais West Peak

Summit Ave.

To Mill Valley

M a r i n   M u n i c i p a l   W a t e r   D i s t r i c t

Old Railroad Grade

Old Railroad Grade

E. Ridgecrest Blvd.

West Point Inn

Old Stage Rd.

Panoramic Highway

Panoramic Highway

To Mill Valley

To Bolinas Ridge Trail

1,500'

Pantoll Rd.

Pantoll Campground

To Highway 1

To Coastal Trail

0   1/2   1
MILE

elevation

2400' — West Point Inn
1800' — Hoo-Koo-E-Koo Trail
1200' — near summit, Mt. Tam Middle Pk.
600' — Pantoll Campground

2   4   6   8   10   12   14
m i l e s

road, climbs initially, but then descends as it traverses around the east side of Mount Tam. Pass by several hiker-only trails, begin climbing at **5.6 miles**, and then at **5.9 miles**, locate a fork. Turn left onto Blithedale Ridge Road and continue the uphill pedaling (or pushing).

Almost immediately, the dirt road reaches a T at wide, dirt Indian Road. Turn left and continue the steep climb. At **6.5 miles**, meet Eldridge Trail at a T. Again, turn left and continue up what's now the north side of Mount Tam's East Peak. This rocky, technical dirt road ascends the peak via a series of long switchbacks. After a long climb which passes by several lesser trails and reveals some wonderful vistas north to Bon Tempe Lake and beyond, Eldridge Trail meets a paved road near the top of the mountain, **9.1 miles**.

Turn right onto the paved road, then quickly find Old Railroad Grade Trail on the left. Take this left onto the dirt road. (To get to the top of East Peak, turn left at the paved road.) Return to the West Point Inn at **10.6 miles**. From here, turn right and coast down the hill to the Pantoll Campground, **12.6 miles**.

DEER PARK ✿✿✿✿

Checklist: 9.4 miles, Loop; jeep trail, paved road
Duration: 1–3 hours
Hill factor: long, steady climb
Skill level: intermediate
Map: *Trails of Mt. Tamalpais*, Olmsted & Bros. Map Co.
Season: year round
User density: medium; cyclists, equestrians
Explorability: moderate

Teaser

The warning about this ride and others in the Golden Gate National Recreation Area (GGNRA), other than the erosion ruts on the Coastal Trail, has to do with deer. Apparently they have a tendency to jump out onto the trail at inopportune moments; a guy from a local bike shop put it this way—"Watch out about getting taken out by a deer." Ouch. Most of the rides in this section contain one or more strenuous hill climbs, and Deer Park is no different. But the amazing views on the ride down and the beauty of the Muir Woods on the climb up more than make up for these hardships.

Descending the Coast Trail with Mount Tamalpais in the background

Views south of the Pacific Ocean

Ride

From the Pantoll Campground near the top of the Panoramic Highway, follow the paved road south, past the park maintenance area. Just after the maintenance building, the road turns to dirt, gradually dropping. Take a left at a fork, **.5 mile**, staying on the Coastal Trail. At **.7 mile**, reach another fork. This time take turn right, following the Coastal Trail to Highway 1.

With all the scenic views available as you drop down the long ridge toward the highway, it's difficult to keep an eye on the tread of the dirt road. **Whoa**, water has eroded treacherous trenches in some sections of the trail and getting a front tire stuck in one would be, well, let's just say you'd rather be a pig on Mount Tam during the eradication. At **3 miles**, reach Highway 1. Turn left and continue down.

At **4.4 miles**, after an awesome, steep, twisting descent on Highway 1, turn left onto Muir Woods Road. At **6.3 miles**, find the Deer Park Fire Trail on the left. **Whoa**, this is an easy turn to miss. The Deer Park Fire Trail, a dirt road that skirts the edge of Muir Woods, provides yet another epic Marin County hill climb. Thankfully, the climb is graced with enormous trees, a soft redwood-needle road, and an even grade as it edges into Muir Woods near the top.

At **8.8 miles**, return to the Coastal Trail—turn right and complete the loop by pedaling up to the paved trail and then back to Pantoll Campground, **9.4 miles**.

DEER PARK

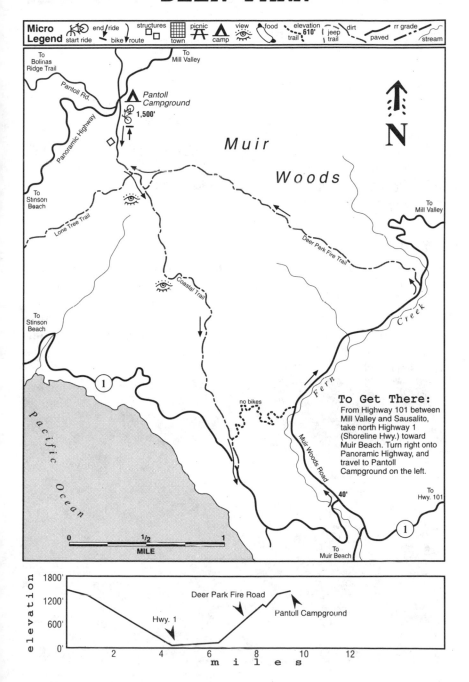

Micro Legend
end / ride · start ride · bike route · structures · town · picnic · camp · view · food · elevation 610' · dirt / jeep trail · paved · rr grade · stream

To Bolinas Ridge Trail

To Mill Valley

Pantoll Rd.

Pantoll Campground
1,500'

Panoramic Highway

Muir Woods

To Stinson Beach

Lone Tree Trail

Deer Park Fire Trail

To Mill Valley

Coastal Trail

To Stinson Beach

Creek

Pacific Ocean

no bikes

Fern

Muir Woods Road

40'

To Get There:
From Highway 101 between Mill Valley and Sausalito, take north Highway 1 (Shoreline Hwy.) toward Muir Beach. Turn right onto Panoramic Highway, and travel to Pantoll Campground on the left.

To Hwy. 101

To Muir Beach

0   1/2   1
MILE

elevation: 1800', 1200', 600', 0'
Hwy. 1
Deer Park Fire Road
Pantoll Campground
miles: 2 4 6 8 10 12

COYOTE RIDGE ✹✹✹✹

Checklist: 9 miles, Loop; jeep trails, paved trails
Duration: 2–3 hours
Hill factor: several long, steep climbs, several pushes
Skill level: intermediate
Map: *Trails of Mt. Tamalpais*, Olmsted & Bros. Map Co.
Season: year round
User density: medium; cyclists, hikers, equestrians
Explorability: moderate

Teaser

The ride from Muir Beach to Tennessee Valley again proves the local mountain-bike adage: If you don't want to ride hills, don't ride in the Bay Area. This ride has a number of long, steep climbs up exposed hillsides. On hot days, be sure to carry and drink plenty of water. (Camelbacks were invented for rides like this.) However, the climbs pay dividends of excellent views and exciting descents. Though only a short section of this rides travels single-track trail, I've rated it four wheels because of the climbing involved.

Climbing away from Muir Beach

COYOTE RIDGE

Micro Legend

end ride · start ride · bike route · structures · town · picnic · camp · view · food · elevation 610' trail · dirt · jeep trail · paved · rr grade · stream

N

Golden Gate National Recreation Area

Panoramic Hwy.

Shoreline Highway

Miwok Trail

Coyote Ridge Trail

Fox Trail
no bikes

Tennessee Valley Trail (paved)

Tennessee Valley Rd.

To Hwy. 101

To Stinson Beach

To Stinson Beach

20'

Muir Beach

no bikes Coastal Trail

Coyote Ridge Trail

Coastal Trail

Pacific Ocean

Tennessee Beach

0 · 1/2 · 1
MILE

To Get There:
From Highway 101 between Mill Valley and Sausalito, take north Highway 1 (Shoreline Hwy.) to Muir Beach.

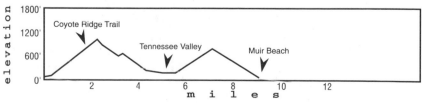

elevation

1800'
1200'
600'
0'

Coyote Ridge Trail

Tennessee Valley

Muir Beach

2 · 4 · 6 · 8 · 10 · 12

miles

Ride

From the picnic area and beach at Muir Beach, find a trail that crosses a short bridge. Turn left just after the bridge, and then quickly arrive at a fork. Turn right onto a dirt road, pass a "no-bikes" trail on the left, and immediately begin climbing up the Coastal Trail. This first pitch is very, very steep and will probably require some walking. The Coastal Trail becomes hiker-only when it exits to the right at **.8 mile**. Continue up the road, which is now Fox Trail.

At **1.7 miles**, reach an intersection. Turn left onto Coyote Ridge Trail and continue climbing. Stay on the main dirt road as you climb the ridge. At **2.2 miles**, reach the top and some spectacular views. When the road forks at **2.5 miles**, turn right onto the Miwok Trail, continuing downhill. At **3 and 3.2 miles**, pass trails on the left. Remain on the Miwok Trail, which begins ascending.

Take a soft right turn at a fork, **3.3 miles**. Soon, the trail narrows and begins dropping into the Tennessee Valley. At **4.4 miles**, reach a trailhead at the end of the motorized section of the Tennessee Valley Road. Pass through a gate, then turn right and ride gradually downhill on the paved Tennessee Valley Trail. Pass by two trails on the right. At **5 miles**, the trail becomes dirt.

At **5.6 miles**, the trail forks. Turn right onto the Coastal Trail and begin climbing. (The left fork goes down to a small beach at Tennessee Cove.) At **6.3 miles**, the Coastal Trail exits on the left and the dirt road becomes the Coyote Ridge Trail. Reach the top of the ridge and an intersection, **7.2 miles**. Go left and complete the loop by returning to the Muir Beach picnic area via a very steep downhill, **9 miles**.

WILDCAT CANYON ✺✺✺

Checklist: 10.5 miles, Loop; dirt roads, paved bicycle path
Duration: 2–3 hours
Hill factor: long, steep hills, some pushing
Skill level: intermediate
Map: *Trails of the East Bay Hills* (North), Olmsted & Bros. Map Co.
Season: all year
User density: high; cyclists, walkers, runners, equestrians
Explorability: moderate

Teaser

On weekends during good weather, Tilden Regional Park and Wildcat Canyon Regional Park are full of tie-dyes throwing disc, parents strolling infants, couples smooching, teenagers drinking, middle-aged professionals running, and old folks shaking their heads at the whole scene. Numerous trails in both parks are closed to bicycles, but many of the dirt fire roads are open and these provide great, scenic riding. Mountain bicyclists have access to most of the fire roads in the San Francisco area, a better track record than the Seattle area where most trails *and* many dirt roads have been closed to bicycles. This ride, rated at three wheels due to the strenuous climb, provides exciting riding and incredible views.

Near the top of San Pablo Ridge

Ride

Beginning from one of the parking areas at the Wildcat Canyon Creek Trailhead, find the start of Loop Road Trail. This dirt road leads to the Wildcat Canyon Trail. (Although Wildcat Canyon leaves from the same parking area, bicycles are prohibited on the first half mile of the trail because it is so congested with pedestrians.) **Whoa**, this first section is confusing, but as long as you stay on designated bike routes and follow the signs for Jewel Lake and Wildcat Canyon Creek Trail, you'll get there.

At **.9 mile**, when Loop Road Trail joins Wildcat Canyon Creek Trail, turn right and head north up the wide dirt road. Pass Rifle Range Road on the left and Havey Canyon Road on the right, **2.9 miles**. Continue straight up Wildcat Canyon to a fork at the **3.1-mile point**. Take the right fork, pass through a gate, and begin a thigh-burning climb up Mezue Trail, another dirt road.

After an excruciating climb up an exposed hillside, reach the top of the ridge at **4.3 miles**. The ridge top affords panoramic views of much of the Bay Area— the Golden Gate Bridge, the Bay Bridge, Angel Island, Oakland, and San Francisco. As you pedal along the ridge, following signs for Nimitz Way, pass two trails that exit back to the left.

At **4.8 miles**, turn right onto Nimitz Way. Nimitz, a paved, non-motorized trail with a 15-mph speed limit, jaunts easily along the ridge. Pass by a trail on the right at **6.6 miles**. One mile farther, pass Laurel Canyon Road on the right. It is closed to bikes, although some books and maps show it as open.

Reach Tilden Park's Inspiration Point when Nimitz meets Wildcat Road, **8.9 miles**. But just before the gate, turn right onto Curran Trail. Back on dirt and descending. At a fork, **9 miles**, take a right onto Meadows Canyon Trail and continue dropping. Complete the loop upon arriving at the trailhead at Lone Oak picnic area, **10.5 miles**.

Alternative

To make this a one-wheel ride, continue straight out Wildcat Canyon at the **3.1-mile point**. The trail, which becomes paved, leads out to Alvarado Park at **5 miles**.

WILDCAT CANYON

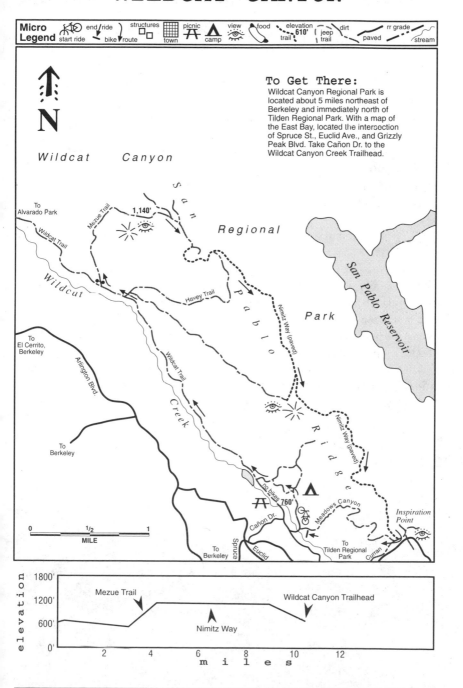

Micro Legend: end/ride, start ride, bike/route, structures, town, picnic, camp, view, food, elevation 610' trail, jeep trail, dirt trail, paved, rr grade, stream

To Get There:
Wildcat Canyon Regional Park is located about 5 miles northeast of Berkeley and immediately north of Tilden Regional Park. With a map of the East Bay, located the intersection of Spruce St., Euclid Ave., and Grizzly Peak Blvd. Take Cañon Dr. to the Wildcat Canyon Creek Trailhead.

N

Wildcat   Canyon

San   Regional   Park

San Pablo Reservoir

To Alvarado Park

Mezue Trail

1,140'

Wildcat Trail

Wildcut

Havey Trail

Nimitz Way (paved)

To El Cerrito, Berkeley

Arlington Blvd.

Wildcat Trail

Creek

To Berkeley

Nimitz Way (paved)

Ridge

no bikes 760'

camp

Cañon Dr.

Meadows Canyon

Inspiration Point

0   1/2   1
MILE

To Berkeley

Spruce

Euclid

To Tilden Regional Park

Curran

elevation 1800' 1200' 600' 0'

Mezue Trail

Nimitz Way

Wildcat Canyon Trailhead

2   4   6   8   10   12
m i l e s

PURISIMA CREEK ✹✹✹✹

Checklist: 13.6 miles, Loop; jeep trails, dirt trails, paved roads
Duration: 3–5 hours
Hill factor: many long, steep climbs, some short walks
Skill level: advanced
Map: *San Francisco Peninsula & Santa Cruz Mtns.*, Krebs
Season: summer, fall
User density: moderate; cyclists, walkers, equestrians
Explorability: moderate

Teaser

The Purisima Creek Open Space Preserve, part of the Mid-Peninsula Open Space District, sits on the Pacific Ocean side of Skyline Blvd. east of Palo Alto. Beautiful and quiet, this preserve is home to redwood, oak, many species of fern, and even open hillsides of chaparral. Despite rumors that all single track in the Bay Area has been closed to mountain bicycles, the single track here, though short, is some of the best on the coast. The compromise comes in the form of a few, not-so-onerous regulations: a 15-mph speed limit, a helmet requirement, and a 5-mph speed limit when passing. This ride has been rated four wheels due to the amount of hill climbing—over 2,600 ft. Call it the hill climber's dream ride.

PURISIMA CREEK

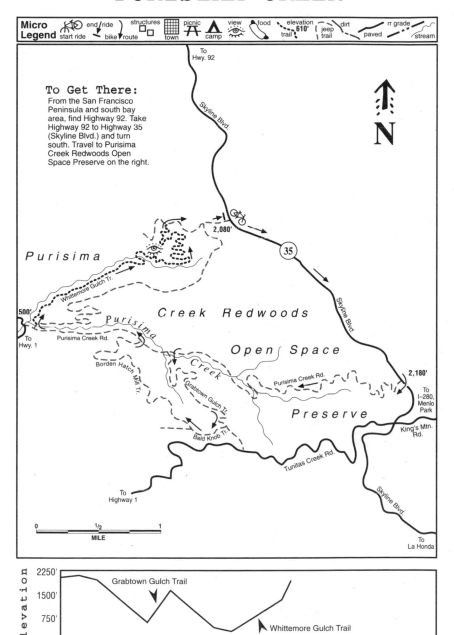

Micro Legend — end/ride, start ride, bike/route, structures, town, picnic, camp, view, food, elevation 610', jeep trail, dirt, paved, rr grade, stream

To Get There:
From the San Francisco Peninsula and south bay area, find Highway 92. Take Highway 92 to Highway 35 (Skyline Blvd.) and turn south. Travel to Purisima Creek Redwoods Open Space Preserve on the right.

To Hwy. 92

Skyline Blvd.

N

2,080'

35

Skyline Blvd.

Purisima

Creek Redwoods

Whittemore Gulch Tr.

500'

To Hwy. 1

Purisima

Purisima Creek Rd.

Open Space

Borden Hatch Mill Tr.

Creek

Grabtown Gulch Tr.

Purisima Creek Rd.

Preserve

2,180'

To I-280, Menlo Park

King's Mtn. Rd.

Bald Knob Tr.

Tunitas Creek Rd.

To Highway 1

Skyline Blvd.

To La Honda

0   ½   1
MILE

elevation — 2250', 1500', 750', 0'

Grabtown Gulch Trail

Whittemore Gulch Trail

miles — 2 4 6 8 10 12 14 16

Ride

From the gravel parking area for Purisima Redwoods Open Space Preserve, pedal south on Skyline Blvd. After a two-mile warm-up and a moderate climb on Skyline, find a trailhead on the right side of the road, **2 miles**. Just north of the hiking-only trail, a fire road begins. Take the fire road, which immediately begins dropping. At **2.3 miles**, the road forks: take the left fork and continue down.

After a dramatic descent, the road reaches an intersection, **5 miles**. For the hill climber's dream, turn left and immediately cross Purisima Creek. Use of your lungs begins in earnest here as the Grabtown Gulch Trail climbs skyward. (If you don't feel like another climb, go straight and pick up the route at the 9-mile point.)

Stay on the main road on the way up Grabtown Gulch. After climbing nearly 1000 ft. in less than one and one-half miles, through redwood forests, reach the top and a fork at **6.4 miles**. Turn right onto the Bald Knob Trail; take a second right at **6.9 miles**, and begin dropping down the Borden Hatch Mill Trail, a wide single track. An exciting and winding descent, the trail joins the Purisima Creek Road at **9 miles**. Turn left.

At **10 miles**, reach a fork: turn right. The route forks again immediately after crossing Purisima Creek. This time, take a left onto the Whittemore Gulch Trail. After a short, very steep climb which may require walking, the smooth single track snakes into a forest of redwood and oak, traversing above a small creek.

At **11.6 miles**, pedal up a series of switchbacks. The switchbacks continue as the trail cuts up the side of an open slope at **12.2 miles**. Lizards scurry across the trail into the chaparral. After a few more switchbacks, the Pacific Ocean is visible over the tall trees, way down the valley.

The single track and the Whittemore Trail end at an intersection, **12.8 miles**. Turn right onto the fire road and begin one of the toughest climbs of the ride. At **13.6 miles**, reach the parking area for the Purisima Redwoods Open Space Preserve to finish the loop.

Single track in Purisima Creek Open Space Preserve

BUTANO STATE PARK ✹✹✹✹

Checklist: 21.5 miles, Loop; dirt roads, jeep trails, paved roads
Duration: 3–5 hours
Hill factor: long stretches of tough climbing
Skill level: intermediate
Map: *San Francisco Peninsula & Santa Cruz Mtns.*, Krebs
Season: spring, summer, fall
User density: moderate; cyclists, walkers, vehicles
Explorability: high

Teaser

The illustration of a Pacific giant salamander on the cover of the Butano State Park map got my attention. Like the ecosystem changes that occur in the Moran State Park ride (page 47), the Butano ride begins in a wet redwood and douglas fir forest, complete with newts and banana slugs, mushrooms and skunk cabbage, then climbs up to oak forests and chaparral hillsides where you're likely to find lizards and rattlesnakes in the small rocks and gravelly soil. Bicycles are not allowed on most Butano State Park trails; this ride follows primarily non-motorized dirt roads. Even though it's not too technical, the distance and climbs force a four-wheel rating. The campground at Butano is beautiful, but watch out for the packs of raccoons that treat the campsites like endless trays of dim-sum.

Climbing along the north edge of Butano State Park

Ride

From the intersection of Cloverdale Road and the Butano State Park entrance, ride north. (If you ride from the campground to this intersection, add 1.6 miles each way, with a 300 ft. climb on the way back.) At **.9 mile**, take the dirt road on the right with a gate just around the corner. Pedal gradually up the smooth dirt road. At **2.5 miles**, pass a trail on the right: No bikes allowed. Continue up the main road.

Pass a road with a gate on the left at **3.7 miles**, stay on the main road, right. After **4 miles** the grade seems steeper as you ride from chaparral slopes into pine and oak forests and back; the road is made of looser gravel. At a false summit, **4.8 miles**, the dirt road traverses with views below of the big-tree forests of lower Butano State Park. At **5.7 miles**, the road levels out again before continuing up.

For the next five miles, stay on the main road which rollercoasters, passes a landing strip, and rollercoasters some more. Don't be tempted by the lesser roads and trails that spur off during this section.

At **10.4 miles**, reach a thick wire across the road. The road immediately intersects with another road—go straight. Reach a fork at **11 miles**. Bear right and immediately pass through a gate. Reach another fork at **11.9 miles**, and again take the right fork that continues down Berry Creek Ridge on the Johansen Trail. This

BUTANO STATE PARK

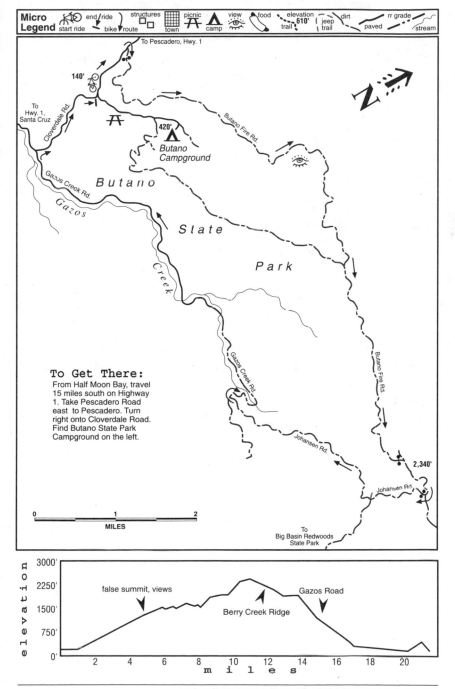

Micro Legend — end/ride, start ride, bike route, structures, town, picnic, camp, view, food, elevation 610', trail, jeep trail, dirt, paved, rr grade, stream

To Pescadero, Hwy. 1

140'

To Hwy. 1, Santa Cruz

Cloverdale Rd.

Butano Fire Rd.

N

420'
Butano Campground

Gazos Creek Rd.

Butano

Gazos

State

Creek

Park

Butano Fire Rd.

Gazos Creek Rd.

2,340'

Johansen Rd.

Johansen Rd.

To Get There:
From Half Moon Bay, travel
15 miles south on Highway
1. Take Pescadero Road
east to Pescadero. Turn
right onto Cloverdale Road.
Find Butano State Park
Campground on the left.

0   1   2
MILES

To
Big Basin Redwoods
State Park

elevation

3000'

2250'

1500'

750'

0'

false summit, views

Berry Creek Ridge

Gazos Road

m i l e s
2   4   6   8   10   12   14   16   18   20

Cruising down Gazos Creek Road

trail parallels the border just inside Big Basin Redwoods State Park. Continue the descent through beautiful forests.

At **12.4 miles**, ride through an open gate. Ignore the old dirt logging road off to the right; stay on the main road. At **13.4 miles**, there's more confusing roads exiting. Stay on the main trail, which kind of bears around to the left and climbs up a hill. At **14.3 miles**, come to a fork. Take the left fork, following the main road.

Reach Gazos Road at **14.7 miles** and take a right. The road descends a a steady pace. When the road becomes paved, bear to the left. Pedal alongside Gazos Creek as it twinkles and winks and clicks its heels toward the Pacific.

At **20.2 miles**, reach Cloverdale Road—turn right and begin a series of steep climbs and descents. At **21.5 miles**, complete the loop at the intersection of Butano State Park.

MORE RIDES

Point Reyes

In addition to the Bear Valley Bike & Hike (page 142), Point Reyes National Seashore has several other trails that bicycles are allowed on. Stop at the Visitor's Center and ask which are appropriate for the time of year you are traveling. One suggestion is the Olema Valley Trail, which parallels Highway 1 south of the Five Brooks Trailhead. The Olema Valley Trail, a relatively flat, sometimes technical single track, provides connections to the Bolinas Ridge Trail and Mount Tamalpais. For more information, call the Point Reyes National Seashore Headquarters ☎ 415-663-1092.

Mount Tamalpais

With the Olmsted map—*Trails of Mount Tamalpais and the Marin Headlands*—in your map case, you can ride hundreds of miles of fire roads across the Golden Gate National Recreation Area (GGNRA) and the other jurisdictions that manage the Marin Headlands. Of course, nearly all the single track is closed to bicycles, but the views, the workout, and often the quality of the land itself is the same as on the narrow trails. Most fire roads in the GGNRA have a posted, 15-mph speed limit. For more information, call the GGNRA ☎ 415-331-1540.

Angel Island

If you can figure out the ferry schedule from Tiburon to Angel Island, you might want to take your bicycle over for a tour around the island. There are plenty of nice spots to picnic, as well as primitive camping. For camping reservations, call MISTIX ☎ 800-444-7275; for more information, call ☎ 415-435-1915.

San Francisco Peninsula

One of the best kept secrets of the San Francisco Bay Area bicycle community is the single-track riding available south of the city on the peninsula. In addition to the Purisima Open Space Preserve, great trails can be found at the Long Ridge Open Space, Big Basin Redwoods State Park, as well as other parks and Open Space Preserves (OSP). Check out the Krebs map: *San Francisco Peninsula and Santa Cruz Mountains*.

AROUND BIG SUR
TO SANTA BARBARA

PRELUDE

Perhaps the most peaceful moment I remember while touring and mountain bicycling the Pacific coast came near Big Sur, just south of Pfeiffer–Big Sur Campground. We left camp early in the morning; fog bathed the redwoods and kept the temperature down as we began the long climb up the west edge of the Santa Lucia Mountains.

For the next 110 miles Highway 1 clings to the side of those mountains, remote and rugged, traversing this windy, hilly road and offering a two-day vista. Forgotten was the struggle of pedaling through the cities to the north; and no thoughts yet of the crowded highways to the south between San Luis Obispo and Santa Barbara.

The fog had begun to burn off as we arrived at Nepenthe—a gift shop and restaurant located at the top of the first summit. It was an expensive coffee and cinnamon bun, but as I relaxed into the canvas director's chair and read *The New York Times*, I could have cared less. It was warm on the patio as the sun broke up the fog, allowing brief glimpses of the Pacific Ocean a thousand feet below.

A week later, I rode up Little Pine Mountain (page 199), in the Santa Ynez Mountains north of Santa Barbara. It was late October, but very hot in the mountains. The flies swarmed. I began riding too late in the day to complete the loop because I had waited for it to cool down. When darkness came, I walked my bike down the steep, sandy single track; I hoped the familiar dirt road that closed the loop would emerge from the darkness of the trail ahead. The air cooled quickly in the clear night. After a while, the batteries in my light failed, and suddenly I was scared: goose bumps stood up on the back of my neck.

I reached the road in complete darkness, exhausted from the fright. I pedaled slowly back to Upper Uso Campground. At camp, I looked up and saw the stars as if for the first time that night. For some reason I thought of sipping coffee at Nepenthe, easing into that director's chair, and staring through the patterns of fog to the Pacific Ocean below.

Whistler

Canada U.S.A.

British Columbia & Washington (p. 34)

Seattle

Astoria

Washington Oregon

Portland

PACIFIC

The Oregon Coast (p. 64)

Gold Beach

Oregon California

California's Lost Coast (p. 90)

Fort Bragg

To the San Francisco Bay Area (p. 134)

San Francisco

Wilder Ranch — Santa Cruz

Monterey

Big Sur

San Luis Obispo

Santa Ynez Mountains

Santa Barbara

OCEAN

TOUR GUIDE

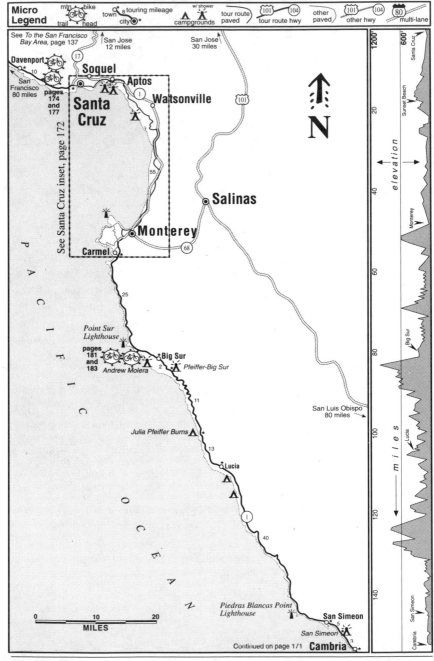

Continued on page 171

TOUR GUIDE

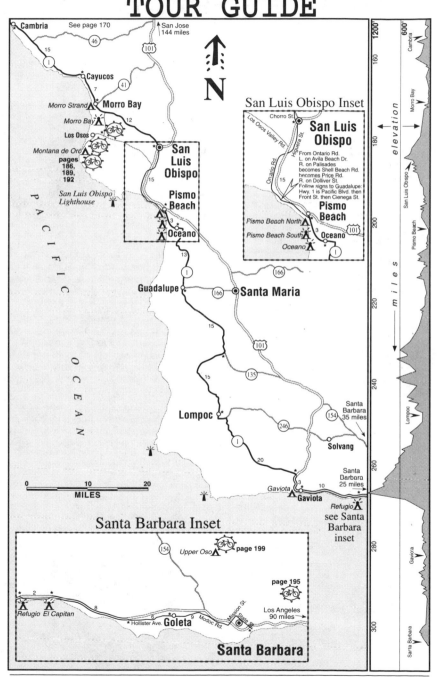

QUICK FACTS

miles (touring south from Santa Cruz, CA)

0   **RIDE:** Some of the best single-track trails on the coast can be found at **Wilder Ranch State Park**, ☎ 408-423-9703, a 28-mile trail system built for mountain bicyclists and equestrians. See pages 174 and 177.

0   **MAPS:** Check out the **Krebs Cycling Maps** for more mountain bicycling ideas near Santa Cruz. When touring, try *Monterey and Santa Cruz* by Compass Maps.

0   **REPAIR:** Another flat? Check out **Another Bike Shop** in Santa Cruz on the tour route, ☎ 408-427-2232.

0   **INSET:** Santa Cruz.

miles (touring south from Santa Cruz, CA)

0   **ROUTE:** The touring route can get crowded in southern California—with all kinds of users, even ones who surf.

20   **CAMP:** The sunsets are perfect at **Sunset Beach Campground**, ☎ 408-724-1266, but the Brussels sprout fields and pine cones that explode in 95° heat are equally interesting.

65   **ROUTE:** The **touring route around Big Sur**—from Carmel to Cambria—is remote and demanding. Highway 1 is narrow and hilly, the cliffs give vertigo, and vehicles sometimes drive too close. But wonderful views and thrilling descents make up for it.

96   **EAT:** Relax under the umbrellas and soak in the views from the deck at **Nepenthe**, a restaurant and gift shop located on Hwy. 1, 4 miles south of the town of Big Sur.

146 **SEE:** Expanding the definition of ostentatious, the famous **Hearst Castle**, located near San Simeon, is worth an afternoon visit.

188 **REPAIR:** Foothill Cyclery in San Luis Obispo, ☎ 805-541-4101.

188 **READ:** In addition to the books listed in *More Rides* on page 203, check out *Mountain Biking the Central Coast* by Carol Berlund.

203 **CAMP:** There are several campgrounds near **Pismo Beach**. The North Beach Campground sits just behind the sand dunes and next to a Monarch butterfly preserve.

279 **WARNING:** The mapped route finishes with a 23 mile stretch on **Highway 101 into Santa Barbara**. This is an extremely dangerous section of road: numerous bicyclists are killed each year. Don't push into Santa Barbara if you are tired or if it's late.

302* **SLEEP:** For those who fall in love with the biking in the San Rafael Mountains, you may stay at the **Ballard Inn**, ☎ 805-688-7770, a fine B&B near Solvang, Calif., a town more Danish than Denmark. The seats on the porch face the mountains, so you can plan the day's route while the innkeepers prepare lunch.

302 **READ: Earthling Bookstore** ☎ 805-965-0926, on State Street in Santa Barbara: helpful, open late, coffee served. Need I say more?

302 **EAT: Cafe Siena**, ☎ 805-963-7344, located on State Street between Earthling bookstore and SBCR, prepares the "best pizza in the world," according to Wade Praeger. Also open for morning espresso.

302 **SLEEP: Santa Barbara Cinnamon Rolls** (SBCR), located at the end of

State Street in the final block of the touring route, is a must for all sugar lovers. Local pigeons have learned a way to procure the tasty buns, so cover your coffee to avoid their poison pill.

302 **SLEEP:** The gardens around **The Simpson House**, ☎ 805-963-7067, provide a taste of what's to come.  From the hand-painted wallpaper to the beautifully appointed parlors, this B&B at first feels like a Victorian museum. But the friendliness of the innkeepers, Glyn and Linda Davies, and their staff will put you at ease; the leisurely breakfasts out on the veranda will convince you to ask about extending your stay. It's a short walk or pedal to Cafe Siena. A shed is being built to hold bikes.

302* **CAMP:** Surrounded by chaparral hillside in Oso Canyon, **Upper Oso Campground** is sparse, but makes for a perfect base camp to mountain bike in the Santa Ynez and San Rafael Mountains (see page 199).

302 **SLEEP: The Olive House**, ☎ 805-962-4902, a pleasant B&B close to Santa Barbara's State Street, is a nice choice when touring.  The innkeeper, Lois Gregg, lives in the house and thus provides great hospitality. The home sits on a hill and affords pleasant views of the area. It's small size—just six rooms—add to the intimate character.

*side trip off tour route

WILDER RANCH–SHORT ✪✪

Checklist: 5.5 miles, Loop; dirt trails, jeep trails
Duration: 1–2 hours
Hill factor: lots of up and down, occasional walking
Skill level: advanced
Map: *Wilder Ranch State Park*, Southeast Publications
Season: all year
User density: high; cyclists, walkers, equestrians
Explorability: high

Teaser

The trail system in Wilder Ranch provides some of the most enjoyable riding found anywhere. The combination of dirt roads and single track, old picturesque corrals and eucalyptus groves make for an excellent experience. There are two Wilder Ranch rides detailed in *Wild Pigs*, but the best thing about this area is the myriad of trails. Be sure to get out onto all the other trails and explore the area. Created especially for mountain bicyclists and equestrians, Wilder Ranch contains trails for all abilities that criss-cross this beautiful area. The ranger estimates that mountain bikes represent about 80 percent of the use. One word of warning: car break-ins are frequent along Highway 1, so don't leave your valuable stuff lying around in the back seat.

Ride

Starting from the parking area adjacent to Wilder Ranch State Park office, ride east, down the hill toward the Wilder Ranch Cultural Preserve. At those buildings, turn left. Almost immediately, the road becomes dirt and passes through a tunnel under Highway 1. At **.5 mile**, reach a fork. **Whoa**, it would be easy to continue straight; instead take a sharp left, uphill. For the next one-half mile, the route climbs steadily up Vaca Trail, a sandy dirt road. Ride across a grassy table, with oak forests ahead in the distance and the bright glare of the ocean behind.

At **1.3 miles**, arrive at a fork in the trail. Turn left onto Old Dairy Trail, a single track. (The road bears to the right and continues up.) After a number of short, twisting ups and downs along the side of a shallow hill, the trail splits into two for a stretch before joining together again.

WILDER RANCH–SHORT

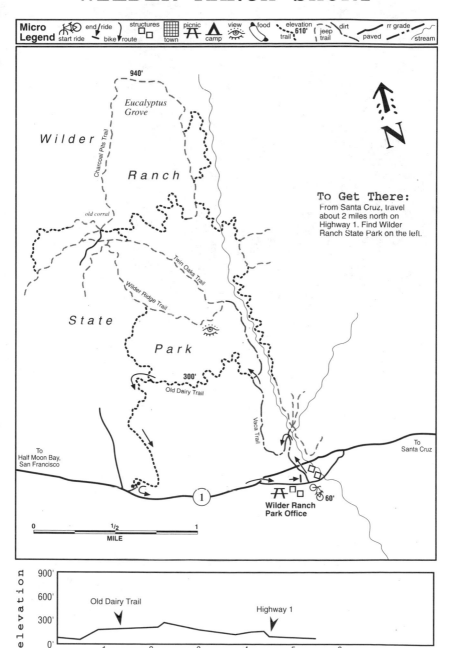

Micro Legend: end/ride · start ride · bike route · structures · town · picnic · camp · view · food · elevation 610' trail · jeep trail · dirt · paved · rr grade · stream

940'

Eucalyptus Grove

W i l d e r

Charcoal Pits Trail

R a n c h

old corral

Twin Oaks Trail

Wilder Ridge Trail

S t a t e

P a r k

300'
Old Dairy Trail

Vaca Trail

To Get There:
From Santa Cruz, travel about 2 miles north on Highway 1. Find Wilder Ranch State Park on the left.

To
Half Moon Bay,
San Francisco

To
Santa Cruz

1

Wilder Ranch Park Office

60'

0   1/2   1
MILE

elevation

900'
600'
300'
0'

Old Dairy Trail

Highway 1

1   2   3   4   5   6
m i l e s

The trail divides at **3.2 miles**. Take the left fork, downhill, which quickly turns toward the Pacific Ocean. Turn left again at **3.7 miles**. After a series of rollercoasters, reach a horse corral and staging area just above Highway 1 at **4.2 miles**. Cut through the gate and drop down the dirt road to the highway. Turn left onto Highway 1, **4.5 miles**.

Less than one mile later, **5.4 miles**, take a right into Wilder Ranch State Park. Follow the signs to the park headquarters and the day-use parking at **5.5 miles**.

WILDER RANCH–LONG ✿✿✿

Checklist: 9.5 miles, Loop; dirt trails, jeep trails
Duration: 2–3 hours
Hill factor: lots of up and down
Skill level: intermediate
Map: *Wilder Ranch State Park*, Southeast Publications
Season: all year
User density: high; cyclists, walkers, equestrians
Explorability: high

Teaser

Here's a rarity: a non-motorized trail system that was actually built for mountain bicyclists and equestrians. Wilder Ranch provides some of the most enjoyable riding found anywhere on the coast. This state park contains 28 miles of dirt roads and trails, which are used primarily by bicyclists. One word of warning: always be sensitive about what you leave in the car while you are riding and especially here, where break-ins are frequent.

Ride

Starting from the parking area adjacent to Wilder Ranch State Park office, ride east, down the hill toward the Wilder Ranch Cultural Preserve. At those buildings, turn left. Almost immediately, the road becomes dirt and passes through a tunnel under Highway 1. At **.5 mile**, reach a fork. **Whoa**, it would be easy to continue straight; instead take a sharp left, uphill. The route climbs steadily up Vaca Trail, a sandy dirt road, then levels as it crosses a grassy table, with oak forests ahead in the distance and the bright glare of the ocean behind.

At **1.3 miles**, pass a single-track trail on the left (see page 174). Continue up the dirt road. The way starts climbing more steeply as the road closes in on the oak forest ahead. The road divides after a steep climb at **2.1 miles**. Take the narrower road—Twin Oaks Trail—to the right. (The climb up the left route—Wilder Ridge Trail—is more demanding, but passes a nice viewpoint.)

Twin Oaks Trail soon becomes a wide single track as it ascends up through the scattered oak trees. At **2.8 miles**, reach a fork in the trail—turn right onto another narrow trail. Arrive at a T at **3 miles**. This time turn left, pedaling slightly uphill. The trail reaches a complicated 5-way intersection at **3.2 miles**. Veer to the right just before the intersection, and then turn right at the intersection onto a road, keeping the dilapidated horse corral on the left.

Pedal up the Charcoal Pits Trail, a dirt road, which ascends at a steady pace toward a grove of eucalyptus trees located near the top edge of the park. After a few steep pitches and curves in the road, the eucalyptus grove will be visible in the distance. The dirt road tops out and then bears to the right just before entering the grove of trees, **4.5 miles**. The road bends to the right again and heads downhill.

Eucalyptus Grove at the top of Wilder Ranch State Park

WILDER RANCH–LONG

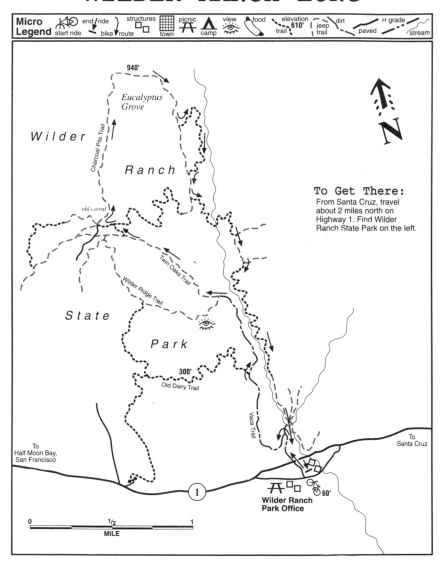

Micro Legend: end/ride, start ride, bike, route, structures, town, picnic, camp, view, food, elevation 610' trail, dirt, jeep trail, paved, rr grade, stream

To Get There:
From Santa Cruz, travel about 2 miles north on Highway 1. Find Wilder Ranch State Park on the left.

Wilder Ranch

Eucalyptus Grove

940'

Charcoal Pits Trail

old corral

Twin Oaks Trail

Wilder Ridge Trail

State

Park

300'
Old Dairy Trail

Vaca Trail

To Half Moon Bay, San Francisco

To Santa Cruz

1

60'
Wilder Ranch Park Office

0   1/2   1
MILE

Whoa, watch for a single-track trail that forks off to the left at **4.9 miles**. Take this trail, which doubles back into the woods. The trail winds and twists, finally emerging from the trees at a dirt road, **5.7 miles**. Turn left, and continue down the road. At **6 miles**, another single track exits the road on the left. Take this trail and follow it down to a stream crossing, **6.6 miles**. The trail switchbacks up and away

Checking out a new single-track trail at Wilder Ranch

from the creek, through a beautiful forest. At **7 miles**, after a hearty climb, the trail ends at a dirt road.

Turn right onto the dirt road. Take the right fork when the road divides. Soon afterward, the road abruptly narrows to a single track, **7.2 miles**. The trail switchbacks down, passing an old rusted truck cab on the way. At **8.6 miles**, the trail widens to a double track and continues down.

Upon reaching a 5-way intersection at **8.9 miles**, turn right onto a dirt road. When the road divides at **9 miles**, continue the level riding on the left fork. At **9.2 miles**, pass through the tunnel under Highway 1. From here, pedal by the Wilder Ranch Cultural Preserve and bear to the right, climbing the hill to the parking area and the end of the ride, **9.5 miles**.

ANDREW MOLERA—BEACH ❀

Checklist: 2.4 miles, Out & Back; dirt roads
Duration: 1 hour
Hill factor: just about flat
Skill level: beginner
Map: *Andrew Molera State Park*, California Dept. of Parks
Season: year round
User density: high; cyclists, walkers, equestrians
Explorability: low

Teaser

There are two trails (roads, really) that mountain bicyclists can use to access the beach from the parking area at Andrew Molera State Park. The route around Creamery Meadow looks nice on the map, but the trail surface is too soft and it soon becomes a walk to the beach. The dirt road through the campground is a better choice. Flat, wide, and short, this is a perfect beginner or family ride.

The campground at Andrew Molera State Park

ANDREW MOLERA–BEACH

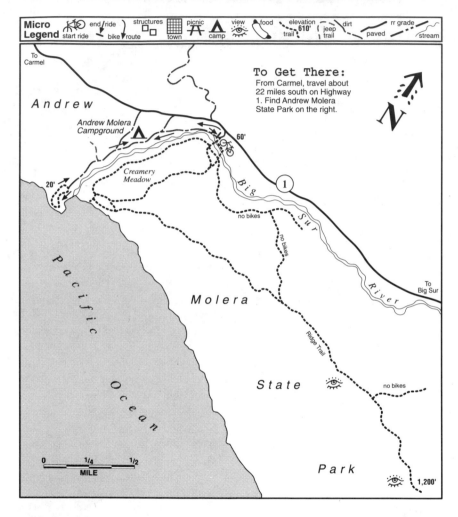

Ride

From the parking lot, bear to the right and locate the wide trail that leads to the campground. The trail becomes a dirt road. At **.3 mile**, pass a dirt road on the right that accesses the highway. Continue straight toward the campground.

Pass through the campground at **.5 mile**. Just past the camp area, pedal through a small grove of eucalyptus. From here, the road descends gradually to a fork at **1 mile**—turn right. The road divides again at **1.1 miles**: this is the beach loop. Take either trail to the beach, **1.2 miles**. Enjoy the beach, then retrace your steps to complete the ride, **2.4 miles**.

ANDREW MOLERA—RIDGE ✿✿✿

Checklist: 8 miles, Out & Back; dirt roads
Duration: 1–3 hours
Hill factor: long steep climb, some pushing
Skill level: intermediate
Map: *Andrew Molera State Park*, California Dept. of Parks
Season: year round
User density: medium; cyclists, walkers, equestrians
Explorability: low

Teaser

It often seems that land managers allow bicycles on certain trails to discourage the use of mountain bicycles. We are guided to the most difficult trails in the park with the hope that we will not return. At Andrew Molera State Park the dirt roads open to bicycles are either too sandy or climb straight up. This ridge ride is one of the latter, a hellish climb up a dirt road. Of course, at the top you are rewarded with an incredible view of the Pacific Ocean and the coast stretching north (if the fog has lifted). But for many riders, this hill climb is just too difficult.

Looking up Ridge Trail, Andrew Molera State Park

ANDREW MOLERA–RIDGE

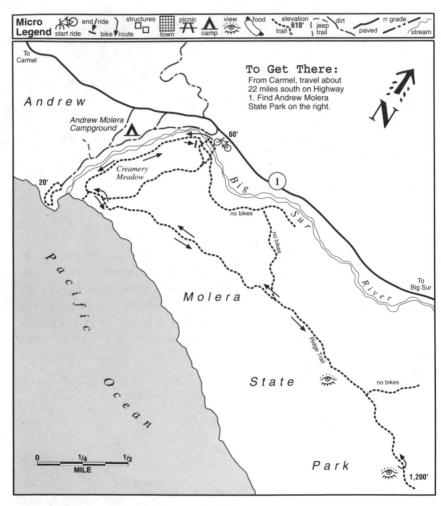

Micro Legend — end/ride · start ride · bike/route · structures · town · picnic · camp · view · food · elevation 610' trail · jeep trail · dirt · paved · rr grade · stream

To Carmel

Andrew

Andrew Molera Campground

Creamery Meadow

20'

60'

To Get There:
From Carmel, travel about 22 miles south on Highway 1. Find Andrew Molera State Park on the right.

N

Big

1

Sur

no bikes

no bikes

no bikes

River

To Big Sur

Molera

Ridge Trail

State

no bikes

Pacific

Ocean

Park

1,200'

0   1/4   1/2
MILE

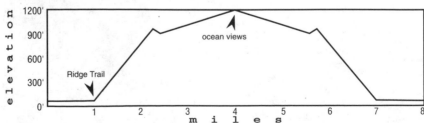

elevation: 1200' · 900' · 600' · 300' · 0'

ocean views

Ridge Trail

miles: 1 2 3 4 5 6 7 8

Ride

From the parking lot, find the narrow bridge that immediately crosses Big Sur River. At an intersection of trails on the opposite bank, bear to the right on the wide, sandy Creamery Meadow Trail. At the **1-mile mark**, arrive at a fork. Turn left and head for the road that climbs steeply up the ridge. (The right fork leads to the beach in 200 yards.)

When the road divides, **1.2 miles**, take the right fork. It's clear that Ridge Trail, a dirt road, is going to be a tough workout. Pass several trailheads from Ridge Trail, but stay on the main road, as the other trails preclude bicycles. The first part of the climb is the worst, gaining over 500 feet in about one-half mile. Most riders will have to walk at least part of this climb. Maintenance crews have dug ditches across the road to channel water off the road and slow down bicyclists. Unfortunately, these ditches are difficult to cross at a slow, uphill pace.

At **1.7 miles**, the road levels somewhat, but the hill looms ahead. After another lung-bleeding climb to a high point at **2.2 miles**, the road actually descends for a short pitch as it enters a grove of oak. As the road winds through the trees, it begins steadily climbing again.

Finally at **4 miles**, after a lot more climbing, reach the top and the end of the trail (as far as mountain bicycles go). The view from the top out to the Pacific and up and down the coast is awesome. After soaking in enough of the view, retrace your steps down the ridge and back to the parking area, **8 miles**. Be sure to keep your speed down on the descent.

QUARRY TRAIL ⊛⊛⊛

Checklist: 4.1 miles, Loop; dirt trails
Duration: 1–2 hours
Hill factor: some steep climbs
Skill level: advanced
Map: *Morro Bay Area State Park*, California Dept. of Parks
Season: all year
User density: moderate; cyclists, walkers
Explorability: high

Teaser

This section of Morro Bay State Park, adjacent to South Bay Blvd., is covered with a maze of trails ranging from technical single-track trails to dirt roads. In the morning, rabbits and lizards scurry across the trails, which are surrounded by grassland and low-growing chaparral. This is a short ride with moderate elevation gain, but the Quarry Trail gets a three-wheel rating because of the number of single-track trails. Still, it's an easy three-wheel ride, even if you decide to explore the many other trails.

Views west, near the top of Quarry Trail

QUARRY TRAIL

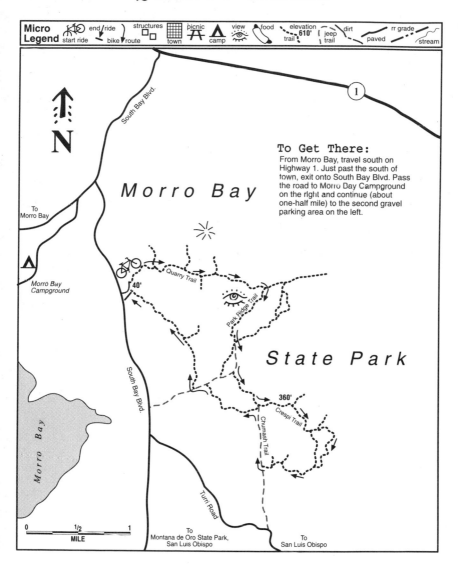

To Get There:
From Morro Bay, travel south on Highway 1. Just past the south of town, exit onto South Bay Blvd. Pass the road to Morro Bay Campground on the right and continue (about one-half mile) to the second gravel parking area on the left.

Ride

From the back of the parking area, find Quarry Trail and take it. The narrow trail winds steadily up, passing through dense chaparral, before emerging into a wide, shallow valley. On the way up, ignore three trails on the left and one on the right—stay on the main trail. At **.9 mile**, Quarry Trail intersects with Park Ridge

Trail. Turn right onto Park Ridge Trail and immediately begin descending.

After a short descent, the trail begins climbing toward a saddle. Reach the top and a 4-way intersection at **1.3 miles**. Continue straight through the intersection, remaining on Park Ridge Trail, a wide single track. Just down the trail, **1.4 miles**, the way divides. Take the left fork onto Chumash Trail. (Park Ridge Trail continues down the right fork to South Bay Blvd.)

But the Chumash Trail hardly gets going before it reaches a 4-way intersection, **1.5 miles**. At this point, turn left onto Crespi Trail, a narrow trail that heads up toward a draw. As Crespi Trail climbs gradually, ignore two lesser trails on the left. Just past the top, **2 miles**, ignore a lesser trail to the right—stay on the main Crespi Trail.

The trail drops, then makes a sharp hairpin turn to the right at a small grove of oak. After the turn, pass several lesser trails on the right. Crespi Trail ends at a T at Chumash Trail, **2.9 miles**. At the T, turn right onto the wide Chumash Trail. Return to the 4-way intersection at **3.2 miles**. Take the unmarked trail on the left, downhill.

At **3.4 miles**, the trail meets a dirt road: turn left, continuing the descent. This is Park Ridge Trail. Almost immediately, though, a single track exits on the right. Take this trail on the right. (If you arrive at a parking area at South Bay Blvd., you've gone too far.) This single track, Live Oak Trail, climbs to a fork, **3.8 miles**. Take the left fork, which drops down to the parking area to complete the loop, **4.1 miles**. (The right fork climbs to a scenic overlook.)

ISLAY CREEK ✷✷✷

Checklist: 9.5 miles, Loop; dirt trails, dirt road, paved road
Duration: 1–3 hours
Hill factor: several miles of steep single track
Skill level: advanced
Map: *Morro Bay Area State Park*, California Dept. of Parks
Season: spring, summer, fall
User density: high; cyclists, hikers, equestrians
Explorability: moderate

Teaser

Other than a technical, two-mile section of single track, this is a relatively easy ride, on dirt roads and paved. But the extended climb away from Islay Creek on single track makes this a tough ride. From the top, nice territorial views of the surrounding hillsides are available. Be cool to the earth and do not skid during the descent. One last thing: I was on East Boundary Trail when an equestrian told me that wild pigs in the area ate rattlesnakes. Though skeptical, I smiled at the image. Later, the ranger was unable to confirm or deny the report.

ISLAY CREEK

Micro Legend — start ride, end ride, bike route, structures, town, picnic, camp, view, food, elevation 610', trail, jeep trail, dirt, paved, rr grade, stream

Pacific Ocean

To Morro Bay, Hwy. 1

N

Hazard Canyon Rd.

Horse Camp

Montana de Oro

Ridge Trail

1,060'

State Park

Boundary Trail

Sponners Cove

Park Headquarters

60'

Islay Creek Road

Islay Creek

To Bluff Trail

To Get There:

From Morro Bay, travel south on Highway 1. Exit south onto South Bay Blvd. Turn right onto Los Osos Valley Road. This becomes Pecho Valley Road. Find Montana de Oro State Park Headquarters on the left at Spooners Cove.

0   1/2   1
MILE

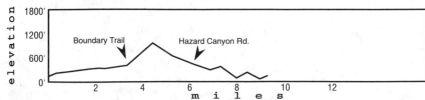

elevation

1800'
1200'
600'
0'

Boundary Trail

Hazard Canyon Rd.

2   4   6   8   10   12

miles

Ride

From the park headquarters at Montana de Oro State Park, pedal west toward the Pacific and Pecho Valley Road. Turn right onto the road and ride north. At **.3 mile**, find the Islay Creek Road on the right. Turn onto this smooth, dirt road and follow it as it parallels Islay Creek.

The road climbs gradually, passing a hiking-only trail and an old barn on the right, and another hiking-only trail on the left. At **3.4 miles**, reach East Boundary Trail on the left, just before the road ends at a "No trespassing" sign. Take this single-track trail, and crank up the twisting, sandy climb. The open, chaparral hillside affords wonderful views. Some walking may be required to reach the top at **4.3 miles**.

From the top, the trail traverses along the side of a ridge, then drops quickly into a stream drainage. Signs of erosion due to the skidding of unskilled bicyclists are evident—be sure not to skid on this downhill. When the trail divides at **5.4 miles**, take the right fork. (A left fork accesses the difficult but popular Ridge Trail.)

Almost immediately, the trail reaches a T. Again take the right-hand trail. Soon after, the trail divides: this time take a left down and continue down the Manzanita Trail. This trail meets Hazard Canyon Road at **6.1 miles**. From here, turn left. Be sure to stay on the main road on the ride down this dirt road to Pecho Valley Road, **6.9 miles**.

Turn left onto Pecho Valley Road, which is paved, and pedal back toward the park headquarters. The narrow road rises and falls as it winds through eucalyptus and oak, affording occasional glimpses of the Pacific Ocean. Pass the entrance to Islay Creek Road on the left at **9.2 miles**. Climb the short hill past Spooners Cove to the campground and headquarters to complete the loop, **9.5 miles**.

BLUFF TRAIL ✪

Checklist: 3.3 miles, Loop; jeep trails, paved road
Duration: less than 1 hour
Hill factor: mostly flat, gentle climb on paved road
Skill level: beginner
Map: *Morro Bay Area State Park*, California Dept. of Parks
Season: year round
User density: high; cyclists, walkers
Explorability: low

Teaser

The bluffs above the Pacific Ocean at Montana de Oro State Park afford wonderful views of the waves crashing against the rocks and a perfect view of ocean sunsets. But perhaps the most interesting sight is the weird rock formations that the ocean has sculpted over years of tidal action. Be sure to stop and watch the artist at work. The Bluff Trail is popular with walkers and runners, so keep your speed down and give these other trail users wide berth.

BLUFF TRAIL

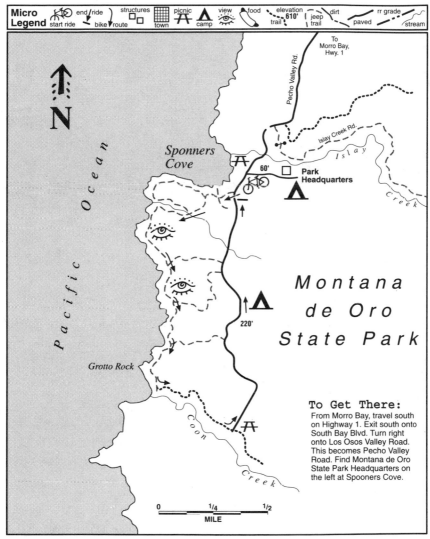

Micro Legend: start ride, end/ride, bike/route, structures, town, picnic, camp, view, food, elevation 610' trail, jeep trail, dirt, paved, rr grade, stream

Sponners Cove

60'

Park Headquarters

Pacific Ocean

Pecho Valley Rd.

To Morro Bay, Hwy. 1

Islay Creek Rd.

Islay Creek

Montana de Oro State Park

220'

Grotto Rock

Coon Creek

To Get There:

From Morro Bay, travel south on Highway 1. Exit south onto South Bay Blvd. Turn right onto Los Osos Valley Road. This becomes Pecho Valley Road. Find Montana de Oro State Park Headquarters on the left at Spooners Cove.

0   1/4   1/2
MILE

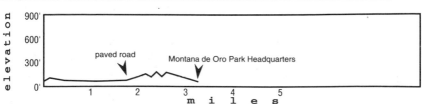

elevation 900' 600' 300' 0'

paved road

Montana de Oro Park Headquarters

1   2   3   4   5
miles

Late in the day along the Bluff Trail

Ride

From the park headquarters at Montana de Oro State Park, which is also the entrance to Spooners Cove Campground, pedal west toward the Pacific and Pecho Valley Road. Turn left onto Pecho Valley Road. Less than one-quarter mile from the start, find a parking area on the right. The Bluff Trail begins from this parking area, **.2 mile**.

The Bluff Trail, a dirt road that skirts the edges of the cliffs, heads west from Pecho Valley Road. Ignore a road to the left immediately after the parking area—stay on the main road. Just after that, the trail divides. Take the left fork. (The right fork heads out to a cliff edge and then loops back.) Soon afterward, **.4 mile**, the trail divides again. Again take the left fork.

At the ocean, the trail bears to the left and cruises along the edge of the bluffs. In addition to the wonderful views of the ocean, weird rock formations channel the waves through holes and into crevices of the rocky bluff. (Or is it the water that channels the rock?) Stay to the right along the bluffs, passing trails to the left that lead away from the water.

But when the trail divides at **1.5 miles**, take the left fork that heads east. As the trail climbs toward the paved road, it narrows. Reach the parking area at the end of Pecho Valley Road, **2 miles**. From here, turn left and ride the paved Pecho Valley Road back to the park headquarters, completing the loop at **3.3 miles**. (Of course, turning around and pedaling back along the beautiful Bluff Trail is also a desirable option.)

ROMERO CANYON ❀ ❀ ❀ ❀

Checklist: 13.8 miles, Out & Back; dirt trails, dirt roads
Duration: 2–4 hours.
Hill factor: long, grueling climb, some walking
Skill level: advanced
Map: *Santa Barbara Mountain Bike Routes*, Santa Barbara County
Season: year round
User density: high; cyclists, hikers
Explorability: moderate

Teaser

One of the classic Santa Barbara mountain bike rides, Romero Canyon is challenging and provides stunning views of Santa Barbara and the Pacific Ocean. The trail ascends more than 2,000 feet over its distance, winding up the chaparral-covered mountainsides. The elevation gain and sometimes technical trail make this a four-wheel ride. Watch out for ticks and rattlesnakes.

Grinding up Romero Canyon Road

ROMERO CANYON

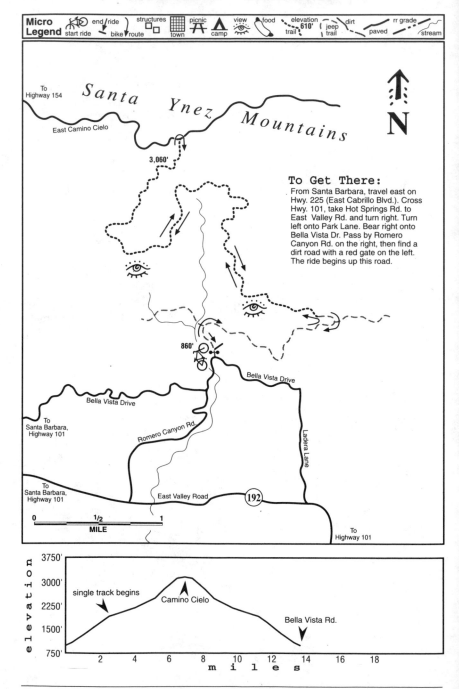

Micro Legend
end/ride — start ride — bike route — structures — town — picnic — camp — view — food — elevation 610' trail — jeep trail — dirt — paved — rr grade — stream

To Highway 154

Santa Ynez Mountains

East Camino Cielo

3,060'

To Get There:
From Santa Barbara, travel east on Hwy. 225 (East Cabrillo Blvd.). Cross Hwy. 101, take Hot Springs Rd. to East Valley Rd. and turn right. Turn left onto Park Lane. Bear right onto Bella Vista Dr. Pass by Romero Canyon Rd. on the right, then find a dirt road with a red gate on the left. The ride begins up this road.

860'

Bella Vista Drive

Bella Vista Drive

To Santa Barbara, Highway 101

Romero Canyon Rd.

Ladera Lane

To Santa Barbara, Highway 101

East Valley Road — 192

To Highway 101

0   1/2   1
MILE

elevation

3750'
3000'
2250'
1500'
750'

single track begins

Camino Cielo

Bella Vista Rd.

2   4   6   8   10   12   14   16   18
miles

Views of the Front Range from Romero Canyon Road

Ride

From Bella Vista Road, pedal up the dirt road behind the red gate. Without warm-up, the dirt road begins a steep ascent away from Bella Vista Road. When the road forks at **.3 mile**, take the road to the right and continue the hectic climb. At **.5 mile**, cross Romero Creek. Just past the creek crossing, ignore the single track on the left—continue up the dirt road.

The road climbs steadily, winding in and out of small drainages on the face of the Front Range. Soon, excellent views of greater Santa Barbara and the Pacific Ocean are standard fare. Pass by a private road on the right. At **2 miles**, the road

A sharp succulent

switchbacks across the face of the mountain, then crosses under a large set of powerlines.

At **2.5 miles**, the road narrows to a wide single-track trail; the uphill traverse persists. Occasionally, the trail is covered in loose rock and scree, and the riding is quite technical. At **4.2 miles**, meet a 4-way intersection: continue straight ahead on the obvious main route. After this intersection, the trail becomes even more technical, and some walking may be necessary (although the views get better and better).

As the trail nears the top, **5.8 miles**, it becomes smoother and not as steep. When the trail forks at **6.4 miles**, take the main trail to the right. From here, the route is more or less flat. Reach the paved road, East Camino Cielo, at **6.9 miles**. After enjoying the view and checking your brakes, turn around here and ride down the same route, making the ride **13.8 miles**. This is a popular trail: watch out for other trail users on the descent.

LITTLE PINE MOUNTAIN ✺✺✺✺

Checklist: 17.2 miles, Loop; dirt trails, dirt road
Duration: 3–5 hours
Hill factor: long, steep climb; precipitous descent
Skill level: expert
Map: *Santa Barbara Mountain Bike Routes*, Santa Barbara County
Season: spring, summer, fall
User density: high; cyclists, hikers, equestrians, motorcyclists
Explorability: high

Teaser

The ride up and around Little Pine Mountain is a long, strenuous trip. A series of relentless switchbacks climb up around the back of the mountain, where amazing views of Dick Smith Wilderness and San Rafael Wilderness are available. The primitive campground near the top at Happy Hollow is a great place to stop for a Powerbar, or the energy bar of your choice. Clearly a four-wheel ride, the beauty and excellent vistas are the reward for much hard work.

Big Pine Road, on the way up Little Pine Mountain

Chaparral hillsides, as the road ascends Buckhorn Ridge

Ride

From the Upper Oso Campground, find the gated road—variously called Big Pine Road, Camuesa Road, and Buckhorn Road depending on the map—that exits from the north end of the campground. After a warning about poison oak, ticks, rattlesnakes, black bear, and mountain lion (they didn't mention the wild pigs), the road begins its steep climb toward Little Pine Mountain. Sandy in places due to the moderate to high number of motorcycles that use this route, the road is sometimes difficult to negotiate as it switchbacks up.

Pass the trail to Pine Mountain at **.7 mile**. The road mounts the ridge and, after several more switchbacks, the road surface is more compact and ridable. At **2.9 miles** (the grade has eased somewhat) pass a trail on the right called Camuesa Connector. Continue up the road. The road divides at **4.5 miles**. Take the left fork toward Buckhorn Road and Little Pine Mountain.

LITTLE PINE MOUNTAIN

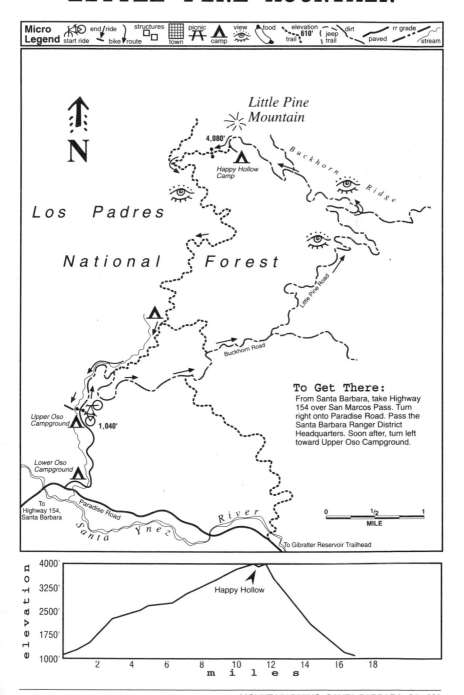

Micro Legend: end/ride · start ride · bike route · structures · town · picnic · camp · view · food · elevation 610' · dirt trail · jeep trail · paved · rr grade · stream

Little Pine Mountain

4,080'

Happy Hollow Camp

Buckhorn Ridge

Los   Padres

National   Forest

Little Pine Road

Buckhorn Road

To Get There:
From Santa Barbara, take Highway 154 over San Marcos Pass. Turn right onto Paradise Road. Pass the Santa Barbara Ranger District Headquarters. Soon after, turn left toward Upper Oso Campground.

Upper Oso Campground   1,040'

Lower Oso Campground

To Highway 154, Santa Barbara

Paradise Road

Santa   Ynez   River

0   1/2   1
MILE

To Gibralter Reservoir Trailhead

elevation (4000', 3250', 2500', 1750', 1000')

Happy Hollow

miles (2, 4, 6, 8, 10, 12, 14, 16, 18)

The road continues climbing at a moderate clip. After a short descent, several long switchbacks route the road across the face of a sheer cliff. The daunting climb is mediated by the amazing views of Oso Canyon and the Camuesa Creek drainage below. Unfortunately, upon gaining the top of the cliff, the road continues up at a steady grade. At **9 miles**, pass by Buckhorn Trail on the right— stay on the main road.

At **10.1 miles**, reach a fork in the road. Turn left toward Happy Hollow Camp. Crest the top at **11.3 miles**, and glide down toward the camp. **Whoa**, before arriving at the campground, find a single-track trail on the right, **11.5 miles**. Take this right, following the narrow trail toward Upper Oso Campground. This trail climbs gently for less than one-quarter mile before reaching a fence. Pass through the fence and bear to the right.

Immediately after the fence, the trail drops precipitously; walking may be necessary. Don't degrade the trail by skidding. At **12.2 miles**, reach a fork in the trail. Turn left and continue downhill. From here, the trail descends quickly toward a primitive campground, Nineteen Oaks. This trail is very narrow, in sections in disrepair, and traverses a steep slope much of the way, so riding slowly and walking are prudent for all but the best technicians. Despite the trail, views of the valley are impressive and the varied flora captivating. Just past **15 miles**, bear to the right, ignoring a trail on the left as you pass Nineteen Oaks.

The trail reaches the road at **16.5 miles**. From here, turn right and glide into Upper Oso Campground to complete the loop, **17.2 miles**.

MORE RIDES

Santa Cruz

Located near Wilder Ranch (pages 174 and 177), Henry Cowell Redwoods State Park contains many miles of dirt roads and trails. For more information, check out the Krebs mountain biking map: *San Francisco Peninsula and Santa Cruz Mountains*, or call the park directly ☎ 408-335-4598.

Big Sur

If you are totally and completely into hill climbing and your local mountain biking scene isn't providing enough juice for the squeeze, try the dirt roads in Los Padres National Forest near Big Sur. These mountains rise over 4,000 feet from the Pacific Ocean in just a few miles. The dirt roads in the forest do much the same. For more information, call the ranger district offices ☎ 805-925-9538.

San Luis Obispo

Many cows graze the hills behind California Polytechnic Institute. But the dirt roads are also used by runners, hikers, and mountain bicyclists from the university as well as greater San Luis Obispo. These roads criss-cross the area and make for fun exploring, as long as it is not too hot. More information on trails in the area can be found in a difficult-to-obtain book titled *Fat Tire Fun: The Mountain Biking Trail Guide for San Luis Obispo County*.

Santa Barbara

There is lots of great riding in the mountains surrounding Santa Barbara on dirt roads and single-track trails. Rides in the Front Range and the Santa Ynez Mountains provide a multitude of opportunities. Many guidebooks and maps for the area help lead the way, including *Mountain Biking the Coast Range, Santa Barbara County* by Mickey McTigue and Don Douglass; *Santa Barbara Mountain Bikes* by Raymond Ford; and *The Mountain Biker's Guide to Southern California* by Laurie and Christopher Leman. Forest Service information is also available at ☎ 805-967-3481.

ABOUT THE AUTHOR

In 1980, John Zilly spent nine months circling the United States on a bicycle. Six years later, after receiving a BA in philosophy from Whitman College and bicycling through Europe, he put fat tires on his touring bike and set out to explore the trails of central Idaho. Those explorations developed into *The Mountain Bike Adventure Guide* (1987) and *The Son of the Mountain Bike Adventure Guide* (1992). A year later he published *Kissing the Trail: Greater Seattle Mountain Bicycle Adventures*. When he's not playing on Utah's slickrock, Zilly lives in Seattle where he volunteers as a trails advocate.

ABOUT THE PHOTOGRAPHER

Wade Praeger is an athlete, scholar, and photographer living in Seattle. He is currently working on a master's degree in environmental history at Western Washington University. His photographs have appeared in numerous publications in Washington and Oregon.

NOTES

NOTES

NOTES

MOUNTAIN BIKE THE WEST
WITH ADVENTURE PRESS

For information about other Adventure Press
books or products, write or call:

Adventure Press
P.O. Box 14059
Seattle, WA 98114
206-343-7729

Kissing the Trail: Greater Seattle Mountain Bicycle Adventures
by John Zilly
ISBN 1-881583-03-1 $10.95 paperback   144 pages
Details 41 mountain bike rides within an hour of Seattle, Washington.

Mountain Bike Adventure Guide for the Sun Valley Area
by John Zilly and Eloise Christensen
ISBN 1-881583-00-7 $8.95 paperback   60 pages
Classic mountain-bike trails in the Wood River Valley and Stanley Basin.

Son of the Mountain Bike Adventure Guide: Ketchum, Stanley, and Beyond
by John Zilly
ISBN 1-881583-01-5 $8.95 paperback   60 pages
More classic mountain-bike trails in central Idaho.

Also available:
Handlebar Map Cases
Created by Cycoactive Products
Simple BarMap, $9.95; BarMap OTG, $19.95
Convenient way to carry *and* view maps while mountain biking.